Employee Rights in Bankruptcy

Employee Rights in Bankruptcy

A Comparative-Law Assessment

Bulletin of Comparative Labour Relations 46 – 2002

Editor: Roger Blanpain
Guest Editor: A.T.J.M. Jacobs

Contributors
Prof. Dr. A.T.J.M. Jacobs
together with
Prof. Mr. R.D. Vriesendorp
Prof. Dr. R. Blanpain
Prof. Mr. W.J.P.M. Fase
Mr. S. Sonke

Translated by Rita Inston

2002
Kluwer Law International
The Hague/London/New York

Published by:
Kluwer Law International
P.O. Box 85889, 2508 CN The Hague, The Netherlands
sales@kli.wkap.nl
http://www.kluwerlaw.com

Sold and Distributed in North, Central and South America by:
Kluwer Law International
101 Philip Drive, Norwell, MA 02061, USA
kluwerlaw@wkap.com

Sold and Distributed in all other countries by:
Kluwer Law International
Distribution Centre, P.O. Box 322, 3300 AH Dordrecht, The Netherlands

A C.I.P. Catalogue record for this book is available from the Library of Congress.

Printed on acid-free paper

ISBN 90-411-1942-6

Kluwer Law International incorporates the imprint Martinus Nijhoff Publishers

Printed and bound in Great Britain by Antony Rowe Limited

Table of Contents

Foreword

A bankruptcy is, and continues to be, a tragic event for the (legal) person concerned and the latter's creditors. Those creditors also include the employees, who were dependent upon the bankrupt not only for their income but also for their employment and social security. In a bankruptcy situation they usually have little to expect in terms of payment of arrears of pay (except for those via the benefit institutions), protection against dismissal, continued employment in the event of a business transfer with a re-start, or participation rights. In an increasingly integrated Europe the question arises of how the legal position of employees in a Netherlands bankruptcy matches up against that of employees in a comparable situation in neighbouring countries: Belgium, Germany and Britain.

As an attempt to provide an answer, in the present study the legal systems of these three countries in regard to the above-mentioned aspects are examined and compared with the situation in The Netherlands. This has revealed that the situation for employees of a Netherlands bankrupt is the least rosy of all. Rooted in the DAF bankruptcy of 1992 with its serious and far-reaching repercussions for numerous employees, the research was intended to establish the basics for a possible change in the regulation of employee rights in bankruptcy in The Netherlands.

The study was commissioned by the Stichting Ondersteuningsfonds Oud-Werknemers DAF [Benevolent Fund Foundation for Former DAF Employees] in Eindhoven and carried out by researchers of the Faculty of Law of the Katholieke Universiteit Brabant in Tilburg. Its provisional findings, presented at the conference on "Employee Rights in Bankruptcy" held in Tilburg on 8 December 1999, were considered and discussed from a variety of viewpoints by participants from all relevant sections of society, such as trade unions and employers' organizations, receivers in bankruptcy, banks, public authorities, politicians and legal experts. The end result is the following report, which we hope will contribute to a better understanding of the difficult issue of employee rights in bankruptcy and stimulate the discussion on improvements.

Prof. Antoine Jacobs (Ed.)

List of Abbreviations Used

AFG	Arbeitsförderungsgesetz
AP	*Arbeitsgerichtliche Praxis*
Arbh.	Arbeidshof
Awgb	Algemene wet gelijke behandeling
B.S.	*Belgisch Staatsblad*
BAG(E)	Bundesarbeitsgericht (Entscheidung)
BBA	Buitengewoon Besluit Arbeidsverhoudingen 1945
BeschFG	Beschäftigungsförderungsgesetz
BetrVG	Betriebsverfassungsgesetz
BGB	Bürgerliches Gesetzbuch
BGBL	*Bundesgesetzblatt*
BSG(E)	Bundessozialgericht (Entscheidung)
BVerwG	Bundesverwaltungsgericht
BW	Burgerlijk Wetboek
CRvB	Centrale Raad van Beroep
CTSV	College van toezicht sociale verzekeringen
CWI	Centrum voor Werk en Inkomen (Center for Work and Income)
DB	*Der Betrieb*
DStR	*Deutsches Steuerrecht*
ECJ	Court of Justice of the European Communities
ECR	European Court Reports
EK	*Erfurter Kommentar zum Arbeitsrecht*
EPCA	Employment Protection (Consolidation) Act 1978
ERA	Employment Rights Act 1996
EuZW	*Europäische Zeitschrift für Wirtschaftsrecht*
Fw.	Faillissementswet
Harvey	*Harvey on Industrial Relations and Employment Law*
HR	Hoge Raad
ILO	International Labour Organization
InsO	Insolvenzordnung
JAR	*Jurisprudentie Arbeidsrecht*
JOR	*Jurisprudentie Ondernemingsrecht*
JTT	*Journal des tribunaux du travail*
KB	Koninklijk Besluit
KO	Konkursordnung
KSchG	Kündigungsschutzgesetz
LAG	Landesarbeitsgericht
Lisv	Landelijk instituut sociale verzekeringen
MuSchG	Mutterschutzgesetz
NAR	Nationale Arbeidsraad

NJ	*Nederlandse Jurisprudentie*
NJB	*Nederlands Juristenblad*
NJW	*Neue Juristische Wochenschrift*
NZA	*Neue Zeitschrift für Arbeitsrecht*
OJ	Official Journal of the European Communities
OK	Ondernemingskamer
RDA	Regionaal Directeur voor de Arbeidsvoorziening
Rn.	Randotiz
RSV	*Rechtspraak Sociale Verzekering*
RW	*Rechtskundig Weekblad*
SchwbG	Schwerbehindertengesetz
SER	Sociaal-Economische Raad
SGB	Sozialgesetzbuch
SI	Statutory Instrument
SMA	*Sociaal Maandblad Arbeid*
SozPIG	Sozialplangesetz
Stb.	*Staatsblad*
SVR	Sociale Verzekeringsraad
TPR	*Tijdschrift voor Privaatrecht*
TULR(C)A	Trade Union and Labour Relations (Consolidation) Act 1992
TUPE	Transfer of Undertakings (Protection of Employment) Regulations 1981
TvI	*Tijdschrift voor Insolventierecht*
TVVS	*Tijdschrift voor Vennootschappen, Verenigingen en Stichtingen*
UWV	Uitvoeringsinstituut Werknemersverzekeringen
uvi	uitvoeringsinstelling
WAo	Wet op de Arbeidsovereenkomsten
Wmco	Wet melding collectief ontslag
WOR	Wet op de Ondernemingsraden
WPNR	*Weekblad voor Privaatrecht, Notariaat en Registratie*
Wsnp	Wet schuldsanering natuurlijke personen
WW	Werkloosheidswet
ZIP	*Zeitschrift für Wirtschaftsrecht und Insolvenzpraxis*

1. Introduction

1. CONCEPT, AIM AND LIMITS OF THE STUDY

In The Netherlands the question whether, in the event of a bankruptcy, employees' interests are really given sufficient weight under existing law has been the subject of discussion for some considerable time. Bankruptcy law imposes evenly balanced consideration of all creditors' interests, leaving only minor scope for giving employees' interests preference over those of the other parties affected. In the wake of the DAF bankruptcy of the early 1990s and the resultant mass dismissal of thousands of employees it has been asked whether there are not good grounds for giving greater weight to employees' interests in the event of their employer's bankruptcy – against the background, in addition, of the general function of "compensating the unequal position" of the weaker party in the labour market that is attributed to labour law. This question was the motivation for the present study and quickly leads on to a lively debate. Does an improvement of the position of employees in a bankruptcy, which would be at the expense of other creditors, also give rise to any other detrimental effects? For example, less willingness on the part of lenders to keep the flow of money open or greater control by lenders over the way in which borrowers run their businesses? With, as a result, slower economic growth and hence a lower level of employment? In a certain sense the issue is one of the interface between insolvency law and labour law, a relationship, which is inevitably also governed by economic patterns.

Any revision of bankruptcy law must, furthermore, be sited in the broader context of a reform of insolvency law as a whole necessitating, in particular, more detailed treatment of the role of *surséance van betaling* [judicial leave to suspend payments in insolvency proceedings]. According to reports, in The Netherlands the restructuring of a company undergoing economic difficulties is far simpler at the bankruptcy stage than during the *surséance* phase.

Countries such as Great Britain (1986), Belgium (1997) and Germany (1999)[1] have been prompter than The Netherlands in undertaking widespread revision of their bankruptcy laws, and the present-day Netherlands Cabinet is currently considering plans in that direction.[2]

In short, there is a great temptation to broaden the debate on the possibilities of giving increased weight to employees' interests to an extent

1. Most of the labour-law provisions of the new Insolvenzordnung [Insolvency Order] were brought into force for the former federal *Länder* on 1 October 1996 (see art. 6 BeschFG 1996).
2. See Bijl. Hand TK 1998–99, 24 0396, No. 126; Voorontwerp van een voorstel van wet (versie 13 August 1999), Annex to *TvI* 2001, 1.

R. Blanpain, A.T.J.M. Jacobs (eds.), Employee Rights in Bankruptcy, 1–4.

where it would quickly go beyond the limits of a brief study. Given the constraints imposed upon us in terms of time and human resources, we therefore opted for a more modest approach for the purposes of the present study. In the last study carried out in The Netherlands on employee rights in bankruptcy[3] the situation in other countries was "left out of consideration for reasons of time and space". It therefore seemed to us particularly useful to scrutinize the matter on a specifically comparative-law basis. For reasons already mentioned, in doing so we confined ourselves to a concrete investigation of the major points of correspondence and difference in the legal position of employees in the event of a bankruptcy in The Netherlands, Belgium, Germany and Britain. The choice of these latter three countries was based on the fact that they constitute the major trading partners of The Netherlands. No system of labour law can be sustainable unless it gives due consideration to the relationship between social costs and the country's competitiveness, and hence takes account of the situation as it exists in the case of the trading partners of The Netherlands. One fact helpful for the purposes of our study is that bankruptcy law *per se* does not differ all that much in the four countries studied, which means that a comparison is within the bounds of possibility even from a formally legal point of view. Between The Netherlands and Germany, in particular, there is a considerable similarity in bankruptcy law of many years' standing, since The Netherlands Faillissementswet of 1896 was modelled on the German example. Bankruptcy law in Belgium differs somewhat from that in The Netherlands and Germany and that in Britain differs even more, but still not to an extent that precludes a comparative-law approach to the matter.

For the most part, the research was carried out in the first half of 1999. Documentation becoming available at a later date was taken into account to a limited extent.

The issues featured in our study are as follows:

- the position of pay claims in bankruptcy (Chapter 2);
- the role of guarantee institutions in the acceptance of liability for pay claims (Chapter 3);
- protection against dismissal in bankruptcy (Chapter 4);
- business transfers during bankruptcy (Chapter 5);
- participation rights in bankruptcy (Chapter 6).

Thus, we have not included pre-bankruptcy *surséance van betaling* [judicial leave to suspend payment of debts] and its foreign equivalents,[4] or the position of the managing director of the bankrupt. Also, the study does not cover all aspects of the legal position (for example, not the obligations that must be observed by the employee in a bankruptcy situation).

3. L.H. v. d. Heuvel, Rechten van werknemers bij faillissement, Alphen a/d Rijn, 1981.
4. Such as the *administration order* in Britain (sections 8–27 Insolvency Act 1986) and the *gerechtelijk akkoord* in Belgium. In the case of Germany the *Vergleichsverfahren* was comparable, but since 1 January 1999 has been consolidated with the *Konkursverfahren* into the *Insolvenzverfahren*.

In view of all the limitations we have had to impose upon ourselves no decisive importance can be attached to our findings in the debate on a reform of bankruptcy law. We are also conscious that our study is perhaps capable of improvement in parts: documentation on the matter in question is not always conclusively self-evident. Nevertheless, we believe that it can offer some useful lines of argument for continued debate on the question of an improvement of the legal position of employees in bankruptcy situations.

2. BANKRUPTCY AND THE FOREIGN EQUIVALENTS

In all four of the countries studied a debtor who has ceased payments can be declared to be in a state of bankruptcy by a judgment of the court, either on his own application or at the petition of one or more creditors.

Bankruptcy is a wholly judicial seizure of the debtor's total assets for execution and distribution between the creditors. The debtor loses control of and right of disposal over his assets, while the creditors lose the possibility of pursuing their claims independently. Instead, the court appoints a *curator* (called *Insolvenzverwalter* in Germany[5] and *receiver/liquidator* or *administrator* in Britain) who takes possession of and assumes control over the bankrupt's *boedel* (called *Masse* in Germany and *assets*, *property* or *estate* in Britain). The *curator* has the task – failing an agreement on composition – of selling off the bankrupt's assets and paying the proved creditors out of the proceeds. In this discharge of debts the starting-point is the principle that all creditors must be treated on an equal basis (*paritas creditorum*), but that principle has been displaced by statutory rules on preferential debts. Furthermore, *boedelschulden* [liabilities or expenses of the estate incurred after the bankruptcy judgment] (*Masseforderungen* in Germany) have to be discharged before all others.

In addition, so-called *separatisten* (see art. 57 Fw.: called creditors with an *Absonderungsrecht* in Germany and *secured creditors* in Britain) can separate out their security from the bankrupt's estate and pursue its realization outside the bankruptcy procedure. A *curator* usually performs his function under the supervision of a judicial authority (*rechter commissaris, Amstgericht* (Germany) and *court* (Britain)).

In Britain bankruptcy law is somewhat more complicated than it is in The Netherlands, since it embraces a greater diversity of procedures. It is necessary to make a distinction at the outset between procedures which, concern individual (natural) persons and those, which relate to companies. Only the latter are relevant for the purposes of our study. Among this latter category of procedures, the one most comparable to bankruptcy in the three other countries is *winding-up by the court*,[6] in which the court first appoints an *official receiver* who must convene a meeting of creditors to designate a *liquidator*. In addition to this British law also knows various *receivership* procedures whereby power of disposal over a company is assumed by

5. Called *Konkursverwalter* up till 1 January 1999.
6. See sections 117ff Insolvency Act 1986.

chargeholders, usually the banks, who appoint an *administrative receiver*. This procedure is more commonly used than *compulsory winding-up* in Britain whenever the intention is merely to reorganize the company by means of downsizing, sale as a going concern or a so-called re-start. In view of the subject matter of the present study we shall also include this reorganization procedure in our assessment.

2. The Pay Claim in Bankruptcy

1. INTRODUCTION

In assessing the regulation of bankruptcy in the four countries studied it is important to distinguish between two categories of debts. The first relates to debts arising prior to the bankruptcy judgment, i.e. debts *against* the bankrupt's estate (*prefaillissementsschulden*, or *faillissementsschulden* for short, called *Insolvenzschulden* in Germany and *debts* in Britain), while the second concerns liabilities incurred afterwards as a result of the receiver's activities, i.e. debts *of* the bankrupt's estate (*boedelschulden*, called *Masseverbindlichkeiten* in Germany and *expenses* in Britain). This latter category also includes those liabilities, which are classed as such by the legislators.

In all four countries studied employees' pay claims relating to work performed *prior to* the bankruptcy judgment are classed as debts *against* the bankrupt's estate. Separate treatment is given to debts *of* the bankrupt's estate in three of the four countries (The Netherlands, Belgium and Germany). This category includes employees' pay claims relating to work performed *after* the bankruptcy judgment. In Britain, on the other hand, in *winding-up* proceedings such claims are never classed as *expenses*; they are classed as debts *against* the bankrupt's estate in exactly the same way as claims arising prior to the bankruptcy judgment. In the case of *receivership* proceedings these claims are covered in a manner comparable to the situation in The Netherlands, Belgium and Germany.

2. PAY CLAIMS DATING FROM AFTER THE BANKRUPTCY JUDGMENT

Pay claims relating to work performed after the bankruptcy judgment fare best (subject to the conditions discussed below) in The Netherlands, Germany and Belgium, because in these countries they are classed as debts *of* the estate, which must be discharged preferentially. Such debts are paid before the debts *against* the estate. They rank first – apart, of course, from the payment of debenture holders and mortgagees (secured creditors).

This high priority given to post-bankruptcy pay claims is not without good reason. It may be in the interests of the estate to continue operating the company for a while,[1] for example in order to complete projects, sell off stocks and so on. Another reason may be to keep open the possibility of selling all or

1. Goode R., Principles of Corporate Insolvency, London, 1997, p. 154.

R. Blanpain, A.T.J.M. Jacobs (eds.), Employee Rights in Bankruptcy, 5–12.

part of the company as a going concern, something, which is usually precluded if its business activity ceases. All this can increase the proceeds from the estate. It is consequently often necessary for certain employees to be retained in employment for a time. If their pay claims were not then given very high priority, receivers would not find any employees who were willing to continue working after the bankruptcy judgment.[2]

However, this high priority also has one drawback: where the receiver has no urgent need of employees he will dismiss them as quickly as possible in order to avoid running up post-bankruptcy liabilities unnecessarily.

2.1 Ranking

The fact that the pay claims in question are classed as post-bankruptcy liabilities of the estate still does not solve the problem of the ranking of these liabilities in the event of a so-called "negative estate" (*negatieve boedel* or *boedelfaillissement*).[3] If there is eventually insufficient money left in the estate to meet all these post-bankruptcy liabilities, to what extent are the employees' pay claims then met? In other words, a question of the ranking of pay claims for work performed after the bankruptcy judgment.

In The Netherlands no direct answer to this question is provided by the law. It is true that in 1990 the Hoge Raad (Supreme Court) ruled that these claims should be given the same ranking as that applied to pay claims among pre-bankruptcy creditors.[4] As we shall see later, however, this position in the ranking is not all that high.

In Germany the ranking of *Masseverbindlichkeiten* is regulated by law (§§53–55 InsO) and employees' pay claims seem to occupy a reasonably high position in it.[5]

In Britain employees' post-bankruptcy claims are not classed as *expenses* (liabilities of the estate incurred as a result of the receiver's activities), a fact which offers no incentive to employees in a bankruptcy situation to continue to work for the company. Consequently, a different formula is adopted instead for this situation, namely, the appointment by the chargeholders, particularly the banks, of an *(administrative) receiver*.[6] This receiver, in the interests of the chargeholders, carries on running the business with the aim of re-establishing it on a sound footing and will often wish to retain a number of the employees. Claims arising from their continued

2. Herman J., De werknemer en het faillissement van zijn werkgever, *Oriëntatiegids*, 1983/1, p. 9.
3. See, on the ranking of post-bankruptcy liabilities of the estate, van Galen R.J., De rangorde onder de boedelschulden in faillissement (I and II), *WPNR* (1997) 6266–67, and Boekraad G.A.J., Afwikkeling van de faillissementsboedel, Deventer, 1997. On the subject of the negative estate, see Verstijlen F.M.J., Waarom kan de curator niet failliet?, *WPNR* (1997) 6275, and van Galen R.J., Een regeling voor het boedelfaillissement, *TvI* 1997/5.
4. HR 28 September 1990, *NJ* 1991, 305.
5. Under §55(1.2) of the InsO these claims must be met immediately after the direct and indirect "Kosten des Insolvenzverfahrens" (§§54 and 55(1) InsO).
6. See section 29(2) Insolvency Act 1986.

employment become the personal liability of the *administrative receiver* (section 44 Insolvency Act).[7] However, in respect of this liability the *(administrative) receiver* is entitled to an *indemnity* out of the estate, which has priority over all other claims.[8] In material terms, therefore, in Britain the status of pay claims dating from after the onset of *receivership* is very similar to that of pay claims dating from after the bankruptcy judgment in the three other countries.

2.2 Amount

The next question that arises concerns the size of the pay claims, which are chargeable to the bankrupt's estate: what is counted as forming part of these pay claims?

In The Netherlands all pay to which entitlement has materialized as from the date of bankruptcy, including the outstanding social security contributions associated with that pay is classed as a *boedelschuld* (post-bankruptcy liability of the estate).[9] Case-law has defined this in more detail: this concept of pay also includes pay during the notice period, travelling costs, holiday bonuses, employee part of the contributions to a pension fund,[10] other funding contributions payable[11] and the entitlement to payment for unused days of annual holiday of an employee dismissed by the receiver after the bankruptcy.[12] Severance payments are dealt with in Chapter 4, Section 6 below.

In Germany employees' claims materializing after the bankruptcy judgment are in principle to be classed as *Masseverbindlichkeiten* (liabilities of the estate). At any rate, §55(1)(2) of the InsO includes, in its definition of "sonstige Masseverbindlichkeiten" (other liabilities of the estate): liabilities from mutual agreements as far as its fulfilment from the estate is requested or has to be realized in the time after the opening of the bankruptcy proceedings.[13]

In Belgium pay claims dating from after the date of bankruptcy constitute a liability of the estate only if the receiver deliberately decides to continue the contract of employment. Where, on the other hand, the receiver decides to dismiss employees (or makes no decision, in which case the contracts of employment are deemed, 15 days after the bankruptcy judgment, to be

7. See section 44(1)(c) Insolvency Act 1986. Also, he is unable to exclude this liability, as emerged *inter alia* in the Leyland-DAF case of 16 March 1995, House of Lords [1995] 2 All ER 65; on this point see also *TvI* 1996/1, pp. 9–10. *Cf.* Fletcher I.F., The Law of Insolvency, London, 1996, pp. 373–378; Davies P., Employee Claims in Insolvency: Corporate Rescues and Preferential Claims, *Industrial Law Journal*, 1994(2), 141–151 at p. 145 and Slade E., Tolley's Employment Handbook, Bath, 1996, p. 250.
8. See sections 37(4) and 45(3) Insolvency Act 1986.
9. See art. 40(2) Fw.
10. HR 28 September 1990, NJ 1991, 305.
11. HR 12 November 1993, *NJ* 1994, 229; *cf.* Tijssen W.P.M., *Advocatenblad* 1992, p. 386 and *advocatenblad* 1994, p. 229.
12. HR 3 December 1999, *NJ* 2000, 53, *JAR* 2000/62.
13. Kania T., Arbeitsrecht in Konkurs und Insolvenz, *DStR* 1996/21, p. 833.

terminated), the final pay claim together with the claim for pay during the notice period is classed as a *faillissementschuld* (pre-bankruptcy debt).[14]

In Britain, in the case of *winding-up procedures* pay claims are never classed as *expenses* (post-bankruptcy liabilities of the estate). This also covers pay during the notice period. They are classed solely as pre-bankruptcy debts. In the case of *receivership procedures* there is the receiver's *indemnity* payable out of the estate, with its associated – high – priority. All contractual obligations regarding pay must be met out of this indemnity, including pension contributions, sick pay and holiday pay. All this applies in so far as they materialize in the course of the performance of the *(administrative) receiver's* functions and relate to work performed after the *adoption* of the contracts of employment by the (administrative) receiver.[15]

3. PAY CLAIMS DATING FROM PRIOR TO THE BANKRUPTCY JUDGMENT

In all four of the countries studied, pay claims relating to work performed prior to the bankruptcy judgment have no unique identity, because they are treated by the receiver as pre-bankruptcy debts. They are settled only after the debenture holders and mortgagees (secured creditors) have been paid and after the bankruptcy costs and expenses[16] have been met. In most cases there is not much left to distribute.

Only up till 1 October 1996/1 January 1999 in Germany was this situation different. There, for more than a 100 years claims arising from the employment relationship of the last six months *preceding* the bankruptcy were classed as *Masseschulden* (expenses/post-bankruptcy debts).[17] This provision gave the German employee as a creditor in bankruptcy situations a much stronger position than that of employees in the three other countries. As from 1996–99 the new *Insolvenzordnung* has put an end to this special position, in that – just as in the three other countries – all claims arising from the employment relationship dating from *prior* to the bankruptcy are now classed merely as claims against the estate and so rank only as pre-bankruptcy debts. This worsening of the position of employees in a bankruptcy situation was partly justified by the protection which the German employee, like those in other countries, has for a number of years received from a guarantee institution covering bankruptcy situations (see Chapter 3 below). Furthermore, the decline in status was offset to some extent by improvements regarding the preference given to severance payments (see Chapter 4, Section 6 below).

14. Verougstraete I. et al., Schuldeisers en ondernemingen in moeilijkheden, Kalmthout, 1994, p. 131.
15. See section 44 Insolvency Act 1986.
16. For Germany, see §§49–53 InsO. For Britain, see section 4.218 of the Insolvency Rules as amended by the Insolvency (Amendment) Rules 1995.
17. See §59 No. 3a subst. 60 No. 3 KO. Nowadays, *Masseschulden* are called *Masseverbindlichkeiten* (see §53 *et seq.* InsO). *Cf.* the comparative-law analysis in Bijl. Hand. TK 1993–94, 22 942, No. 6, p. 24.

Although their status as pre-bankruptcy debts means that pay claims dating from prior to the bankruptcy judgment will usually be recovered only to the extent of a limited proportion, in the other three countries such claims do still enjoy some degree of priority. It is only in Germany that, with the introduction of the new *Insolvenzordnung*, all preferences have been abolished. In the legislation in Belgium, Britain and The Netherlands pay claims are accorded a greater or lesser degree of preference signifying that they rank ahead of ordinary creditors. It should, however, be noted in this connection that these pay claims often share their preference with other preferential creditors (with sometimes even a higher priority), which again reduces the chances of their being met in full.

In Belgium[18] legal costs, funeral expenses, the costs of a final year's illness and the special preferential claims[19] are first deducted from the assets before it is the turn of general preferential claims, which include the pay claims of the employee, subject to a ceiling of 7500 Euro. Next come the claims of the Sluitingsfonds [Redundancy Payments Fund], employees' holiday-allowance claims for the current and past year of employment, claims arising from industrial accidents, social security contributions, other preferential claims and then ordinary claims, which include employees' other pay claims.

In Britain[20] goods, which are subject to the security rights of a *fixed* or *floating charge* represent no recovery value for any creditors other than the *chargee*. The remaining assets are used first of all for the discharge of *preferential debts*, all placed on an equal footing.[21] This category includes *inter alia* tax debts, social security contributions, pension scheme contributions and also outstanding remuneration for the last four months before the bankruptcy judgment subject to a monetary limit of £800 per employee.[22] The concept of remuneration here also includes holiday-pay claims and the legislatively guaranteed continued payment of pay during periods when no work is done and paid time off.[23] It is after this that ordinary claims get their chance. This category takes in the employees' other pay claims, including entitlements to pay for the notice period.

In The Netherlands priority for a claim, other than by debenture or mortgage, can exist only on the basis of law (art. 3:278 BW [Civil Code]). For some cases where priority derives from a preferential right the Civil Code can be consulted.[24] Other preferential rights (particularly those governed by public

---

18. See art. 19 Hypotheekwet; *cf.* Rasschaert K., Veys F. and van Hoogenbemt H., in: Faillissement & Gerechtelijk Akkord: Het nieuwe recht, Kluwer Belgium 1998, p. 249; Herman J., *loc. cit.*, p. 7; see Dirix, *TPR* 98–99.
19. See art. 26 Hypotheekwet.
20. *Cf.* the comparative-law assessment in Bijl. Hand. TK 1993–94, 22 942, No. 6, p. 22.
21. See section 386 Insolvency Act 1986 as last amended by the Insolvency Act and its schedule 6.
22. Davies P., *loc. cit.* at p. 143; Slade E., *op. cit.*, p. 244; Harvey on Industrial Relations and Employment Law, Division G (Insolvency), No. 21 and Smith I., Industrial Law, London, p. 185.
23. Fletcher I.F., *op. cit.*, p. 800; Harvey, *ibid*, p.14. On redundancy payments, see Chapter 4, Section 6 below.
24. See sections 3.10.2, 3.10.3, 8.3.3 and 8.8.5 BW.

law) are not always so easy to find, with the result that practice tends to content itself with using the various preference systems that are common currency.[25] Generally speaking, the order of recourse – apart from *separatisten* (secured creditors) and after deduction of the bankruptcy costs – comes down to a priority for the tax authorities[26] and social security.[27] Next to be met come a number of special preferential claims,[28] after which the general preferential claims have their turn.[29] Claims falling under this latter heading include the costs of making the bankruptcy petition, the financing of pension obligations, and also employees' pay claims for the current and the previous calendar year and claims associated with termination of the contract of employment (Art. 3:288 (e) BW).[30] Last in turn come the ordinary claims, including the employees' other pay claims.

A bill sent to parliament in 1992[31] proposes that in future employees' pay claims dating from not more than one year before the bankruptcy judgment will fare better with respect to tax and social security, since in the draft art. 3:280(5) BW they are placed on an equal footing. Although this is only a relatively small improvement in position, it is not entirely without significance since it would also carry over into the ranking of *boedelschulden* (post-bankruptcy liabilities of the estate). Whether it will actually come to that is, however, unclear, since discussion of the Bill has been held up for some considerable time (since 1994), mainly as a result of the controversy over the "super-preference" given to the tax authorities and their special right of recourse to recovery (art. 3:286–87(draft) BW).

4. COMPARISON OF THE SIGNIFICANCE OF THE RANKING OF PAY CLAIMS IN BANKRUPTCY

It is evident from what has been said above that in all four of the countries studied, by and large, the employees in a bankruptcy situation are in a shaky position as regards their pre-bankruptcy pay claims. Given that these claims constitute pre-bankruptcy debts, they can be met only after all post-bankruptcy liabilities (or expenses) of the estate have been paid. In most bankruptcies, however, by then there are no assets left to distribute. In The Netherlands statistics show that 97% of the pre-bankruptcy-debts simply cannot be recovered whatever the legal preferences are. If this picture is true for

25. See, for example, the still largely up-to-date review by Stein H. in *Advocatenblad* 1994/18, pp. 806 *et seq*., revised to some extent in *Advocatenblad* 1995/5, pp. 194 *et seq*.
26. See art. 21 Invorderingswet 1990 [Debit Enforcement Act]. The tax authorities' special right of recovery with respect to the main assets of third parties in accordance with art. 22(3) of the Act is not considered here.
27. See art. 1(c) Organization of Social Insurance Act.
28. Namely, preferential rights with respect to certain goods (art. 3:280 subst. arts. 3:283–287 BW).
29. See art. 3:281 subst. 288–289 BW. These provisions, amending the former art. 1195, implement *inter alia* the rule from HR 23 May 1980, *NJ* 1980, 502 (Nebig/Nolen).
30. *Cf*. Loesberg E., De werknemer en zijn insolvente werkgever (I), *TvI*, 1998/4, p. 70.
31. Bill 22942.

the other countries as well then the differences in the legal situation with preferences are most of the time irrelevant.

In the exceptional cases in which there are still assets left over after secured creditors and post-bankruptcy liabilities have been satisfied, in three of the four countries studied employees' pay claims may enjoy a certain preference with respect to the other creditors. More often than not, however, they have to share this priority status with other preferential creditors and the priority is not unlimited. In Belgium and Britain only a relatively small proportion of the pay claim (a maximum of 7500 Euro/four months with a ceiling of £800) is given high priority.

In The Netherlands a more substantial proportion of the pay claim is given preferential status (a good one year's preference for the pay claim without any monetary ceiling). However, this preference ranks low on the scale of preferences (after, in particular, tax debts and social security contributions). Consequently this preference does not result in any payment of pre-bankruptcy debts of employees, even is there are assets.

In Germany there is no longer any ranking of preferences. This means on the one hand, that employees are left to compete in the general pool of all creditors with the result that they never will recover much of their claim, but on the other hand they will always recover something, however futile.

As regards pay claims for work performed after the bankruptcy judgment, employees both in The Netherlands and in Germany are in a strong position. In these countries their claims are classed as *boedelschulden* or *Masseverbindlichkeiten* (post-bankruptcy expenses) and must be met before the pre-bankruptcy creditors receive anything. However, since in the event of a "negative" estate with insufficient assets the ranking of the pre-bankruptcy debts (*faillissementschulden*) is still retained, these pay claims would appear to be in a weaker position in The Netherlands than in Germany.

In Belgium the situation is comparable to that in Germany and The Netherlands as far as it concerns the pay claims of those employees retained in employment on the decision of the receiver in a bankruptcy. Other employees are denied this advantage, which means that their pay claims for the period subsequent to the date of bankruptcy are classed only as pre-bankruptcy debts. On the one hand this means that those claims can hardly ever been met, but on the other hand: this category of workers (which after bankruptcy have not been retained in employment) will not have much post-bankruptcy claims!

In British bankruptcy law, pay claims dating from after the bankruptcy judgment are not classed as post-bankruptcy liabilities of the estate (*expenses*), with the result that they have no preferential status. This means that the British bankruptcy procedure is not conducive to the continued operation of the business. Consequently, in such situations it is necessary in Britain to have recourse to the *(administrative) receiver* procedure, which gives the employees more chance of having their pay claims met since they are able to institute legal proceedings against the *(administrative) receiver* (and the banks behind him) on the grounds of personal liability for such claims.

The overall conclusion therefore is, that – irrespective the diversity in the legal rules – the post-bankruptcy claims of employees in bankruptcy situations in all the four countries studied have an equally strong standing, but that the pre-bankruptcy claims of the employees are overwhelmingly left unpaid.

This situation caused the legislators in Europe in the 1960s and 1970s to decide that at least a proportion of these pay entitlements should be paid from collective funds, as a form of social security scheme. This phenomenon is discussed in the following chapter.

3. Acceptance of Liability for Pay Claims by Guarantee Institutions

1. INTRODUCTION AND REVIEW OF THE GUARANTEE SCHEMES

In a bankruptcy situation the secure livelihood of employees can very quickly become jeopardized if they are no longer able to receive their pay. When in the 1960s and 1970s, in the context of a wave of new bankruptcies, it became evident in the countries studied that the traditional protection provided under bankruptcy law (see Chapter 2 above) was rather mediocre, legislation was gradually passed in these countries to provide employees with a new form of income protection which goes further than giving general preference to pay claims in the event of bankruptcy. This happened first in Belgium (1967), soon followed by The Netherlands (1968), Germany (1974) and Britain (1975),

The characteristic feature of this new protection was that it no longer relied on the preferential status of the pay claims of employees in a bankruptcy situation as originated in the 19th century but provided a new form of protection inspired by the more 20th century concepts of social security: employee's pay claims would in insolvency situations be met from an independent fund financed by contributions to be paid by employers and/or employees and /or the state. The fund would then take over the employees' pay claims through subrogation. This new concept was intended to ensure that employees in a bankruptcy situation are more certain of recovering a greater proportion of their claims, with less delay, than they would on the basis of bankruptcy law.

So successful was the new concept that in 1980 the EC legislators decided to adopt it for the whole of the EC: Directive 80/987[1] relating to protection of employees in the event of their employer's insolvency, which requires the Member States to set up "guarantee institutions" to "guarantee ... payment of employees' outstanding claims ... relating to pay". The concept found a following even at world level, as indicated by the ILO's Convention of 1992 on the subject.[2] However, whereas the ILO Member States are not bound actually to incorporate the concept into their national legislation, the EC Member States are indeed under an obligation as from 20 October 1983 to implement Directive 80/987. Failure to comply can render a Member State liable to pay damages to the employees concerned.[3] Directive 80/987 had the

1. Council Directive 80/987/EEC [1980] OJ L283/23.
2. ILO Protection of Workers' Claims Convention No. 173, 1992.
3. ECJ Joined Cases C-6 and C-9/90 *Francovich (No. 1)* and *Bonifaci v. Italy* [1991] ECR I-5357.

R. Blanpain, A.T.J.M. Jacobs (eds.), Employee Rights in Bankruptcy, 13–22.

primary objective of making the implementation of rules of this nature mandatory throughout the whole of the EC territory. However, it brought only a partial standardization of the legislation on the matter already in force in different Member States, since it allowed diverse versions of the concept that had in the meantime been successfully established within the EC countries to continue to exist alongside each other.

Belgium had been the "model country" in this respect. Its Law of 28 July 1966[4] (hereinafter *Sluitingswet '66*) had long before given employees a legal right to a *sluitingsvergoeding* [redundancy payment in the event of company closure]. A year later these provisions were supplemented by the Law of 30 June 1967[5] (hereinafter *Sluitingswet '67*), which provides for the disbursement of certain payments to employees affected by a company closure in cases where the employer defaults on his liabilities. In such situations the *Fonds tot vergoeding van de in geval van sluiting van ondernemingen ontslagen werknemers* [Fund for the compensation of employees dismissed in the event of company closure] (hereinafter *Sluitingsfonds*) stands surety for monetary liabilities of the employer's side, which have not been met. A Royal Decree of 6 July 1967[6] specifies *in concreto* the payments concerned and the ceilings imposed for them.

The model of Belgium's Sluitingswet '67 was quickly followed by The Netherlands in 1968, when a special Title was introduced into its Werkloosheidswet [Unemployment Insurance Act].[7] This scheme provided that from then on the unemployment insurance funds and institutions[8] would stand guarantor for employees' pay claims against an employer in a state of inability to pay. The necessary sums are drawn from the *Algemeen Werkloosheidsfonds* [General Unemployment Fund]. From a systematic point of view this scheme is really out of place in the Werkloosheidswet, since the starting-point of this Act is a "right to benefits", which does not, strictly speaking, apply so long as the employee is still able to assert an entitlement to pay.[9] However, it was decided that this form of welfare needed to be inserted as Title IV of the Werkloosheidswet for functional considerations, owing to its affinity with the subject-matter dealt with there and the legislators' wish, at the time, to place these provisions in the hands of the industrial insurance associations.

In Germany a similar scheme was adopted in 1974 through the insertion of §§141a-n into the Arbeitsförderungsgesetz (AFG).[10] In 1998 this scheme was transferred to §§183–189 of Book III of the Sozialgesetzbuch (SGB), regulating

4. *BS*, 2-7-1966.
5. *BS*, 13-7-1967.
6. *BS*, 13-7-1967.
7. Law of 10 July 1968, *Stb.* 1968, 375. These provisions were subsequently amended a number of times, notably by the Law of 6 November 1986, *Stb.* 1986, 566.
8. Up till 1996 these were the industrial insurance associations, which in that year were replaced by the executive agencies (*uvi's*) coming under the Landelijk instituut sociale verzekeringen [*Lisv*, i.e. National Institute for Social Insurance]. In 2002 this system of uvi's and Lisv has been replaced by the UWV (Uitvoeringsinstituut Werknemersverzekeringen).
9. Sociale verzekeringswetten Kluwer 12, WW toelichting suppl. 90, March 1998, Art. 61–7.
10. Law of 25-6-1969 (*BGBL*, I 582).

the right to what is called *Insolvenzgeld*.[11] Applications for entitlement to this guarantee payment have to be made to the (local) employment offices, which form part of the Federal Employment Service (*Bundesanstalt für Arbeit*).

In Britain a guarantee scheme has existed since 1975, which in 1978 was carried over into the Employment Protection (Consolidation) Act (EPCA) and some time later (in 1996) into sections 182–190 of the Employment Rights Act 1996 (ERA). In Britain employees must lodge their claims with the Secretary of State for Employment, who administers the National Insurance Fund from which the employees' claims are paid.

Because in 1980 Belgium, The Netherlands, Germany and Britain already possessed the guarantee facilities prescribed by Directive 80/987, and because the Directive had been formulated so broadly that their existing national legislation grafted onto it seamlessly, after 1980 these four countries did not adjust their legislation to the Directive beyond changing a few details here and there.[12] As a result, the national systems of legislation on the matter still differ from each other as regards certain specifics. These differences are examined in detail in the following sections, which focus in turn on the differences regarding the scope of the guarantee schemes (Section 2), limitations on the liabilities of guarantee institutions (Section 3) and forms of financing and recovery (Section 4). To conclude, Section 5 gives a comparison of the role of the guarantee institutions in bankruptcy situations.

2. SCOPE OF THE GUARANTEE SCHEMES

The Directive and the national schemes are reasonably broad in scope since they cover any "state of insolvency" of the employer.[13] The broader definition of all situations of inability to pay on the part of the employer as regards the payment of employees' pay is rather crucial for the period when no bankruptcy judgment has yet been pronounced.[14] However, since the present study is confined to situations where the employer has been adjudged bankrupt in formal legal terms, these issues are left out of consideration. In any event, in bankruptcy situations such an inability to pay is always presumed to exist.[15] What is certainly of relevance to the present study is the possibility opened up

12. In regard to The Netherlands: van Haersholte J., Uitvoering EG-Richtlijnen in Nederland, 1958–94, The Hague, 1995, p. 151; in regard to Britain: Burrows N., European Social Law, Wiley, 1996, p. 236.
13. *Cf.* Articles 1 and 2 of the Directive. In Britain the guarantee arrangements apply both to the actual winding-up procedure and to receivership procedures: see section 187 ERA; *cf.* Harvey on Industrial Relations and Employment Law, Division G (Insolvency), No. 13.
14. *Cf.*, in regard to The Netherlands for example, CRvB 31 August 1978, WW 1977/708, *RSV*, 1978/352; CRvB 30 January 1990, WW 1989/63, *RSV*, 1990/269; and notably CRvB 15 December 1993, RSV 1994, 168, which rejected application of the guarantee scheme in situations of judicial leave to suspend payment of debts.
15. Sociale verzekeringswetten Kluwer 12, WW toelichting suppl. 90, March 1998, Art. 61–10.

by the Directive of excluding certain categories of employees from the scope of insolvency arrangements.[16]

Otherwise, because it uses the term "employment relationships" the Directive has the effect that forms of employment, which have no basis in a legal contract of employment, can also be covered. This means that atypical workers can also possibly benefit from the guarantee institutions.[17]

Under the law of The Netherlands the question has risen whether the guarantee scheme would operate in the event of the expiry of fixed-term contracts of employment[18] or in that of judicial rescission of the employment contract on the basis of art. 7:685 BW[19], because the text of the Dutch law (art. 64 WW) states that the scheme applies in the event of *opzegging* (unilateral termination of the employment relationship). Although this concept was initially given a narrow interpretation by the Centrale Raad van Beroep (Central Appeal Tribunal), this Tribunal pointed out that the agencies were permitted to equally apply the guarantee scheme to judicial rescission situations and the expiry of fixed-term contracts, which is standing practice now.[20]

3. LIMITATION OF THE GUARANTEE INSTITUTIONS' LIABILITY

Precisely what elements all fall under the heading of employees' claims relating to pay is an important issue. The Directive gives no provisions regarding the definition of the concept of pay. Indeed, it states that it is without prejudice to national law as regards the definition of terms such as "pay".[21]

In accordance with the Directive the Member States are able to limit the coverage by the guarantee institutions of employees' outstanding pay claims primarily in relation to a specified date: only claims arising prior to that date need be covered. In choosing the relevant date the Member States have three options:

(a) the date of the onset of employer's insolvency,
(b) that of the notice of dismissal issued on account of insolvency or
(c) that of the onset of insolvency or that on which the employment relationship was discontinued.[22]

Next, the Member States are also able to limit the guarantee institutions' payment liability to three months if they have chosen option (a) or (b) or to

16. Article 1(2) of the Directive. Britain has taken advantage of this with respect to seafarers and self-employed partners in a venture. The Netherlands has applied the exclusion to some domestic workers; *cf.* EC Commission, COM(95) 164 final, 15.06.1995, pp. 6 and 8 respectively.
17. EC Commission, COM(95) 164 final, 15.06.1995, pp. 22–25.
18. CRvB 2 February 1993, RSV 1993/142.
19. CRvB 27 October 1992, RSV 1993/100.
20. See SVR Report op 11 December 1991 (A 92/3, Hoofdstuk IV WW). The successor of the SVR, the CTSV (Social Insurance Supervisory Board) has accepted this practice.
21. See Article 2(2) of the Directive.
22. Article 3 of the Directive.

eight weeks if they have chosen option (c).[23] Lastly, they can set a ceiling for the outstanding pay claims that must be met.[24] In these different variants the use of arrangements already in force in Belgium, The Netherlands, Germany and Britain as sources of inspiration for the Directive is clearly recognizable.

Germany's legislation obviously served as a model for the first variant of Article 3 of the Directive.[25] It limits the guarantee of outstanding pay claims to a maximum of three months, meaning in principle the last three months preceding the initiation of bankruptcy proceedings (§183 SGB III).[26] These pay claims cover everything actually owed by the employer to the employee by virtue of the contract of employment (§183 SGB III), therefore also holiday bonuses[27] and the reimbursement of expenses and travel costs.[28] The guarantee, however, does not cover claims, which the employee acquires by appealing against dismissal or any entitlements deriving from a "social plan".[29]

The Netherlands legislation evidently served as a model for the second variant of Article 3 of the Directive. The claims it deems eligible for guaranteed payment are those relating to:

(a) pay for a maximum of 13 weeks immediately preceding the date of termination of the employment relationship.[30] "Pay" is traditionally understood to include broadly everything actually owed by the employer to the employee by virtue of the contract of employment,[31] such as a thirteenth-month's pay (pro rata), compensation for removal costs, essential use of credit cards,[32] compensation for the loss of a company car,[33] necessary legal costs,[34] and so forth;[35]
(b) pay for the notice period, limited to the period of notice specified in article 40(1) Fw.,[36] so to a maximum of 6 weeks pay;
(c) holiday pay and holiday bonuses for one year preceding the date of termination of the employment relationship.

---

23. Article 4(2) of the Directive.
24. Article 4(3) of the Directive.
25. EC Commission, COM(95)164 final, 15.06.1995, p. 26.
26. Strictly speaking, however, this is not necessarily so, because some claims from long before the bankruptcy judgment fall within the scope of *Insolvenzgeld*. Payment can of course be prevented by the lapse of rights and limitation periods.
27. For three months preceding the initiation of bankruptcy proceedings.
28. Schaub G., Arbeitsrechts-Handbuch, Munich, 1996, p. 797.
29. See §184 SGB III; Jacobs A.T.J.M., Inleiding tot het Duitse arbeidsrecht, Arnhem, 1993, p. 65.
30. Art. 64(a/b) WW.
31. CRvB, 5 January 2000, RSV 2000, 238.
32. CRvB, 30 June 1992, *RSV* 1993/19.
33. CRvB, 18 March 1988, WW 1987/298, not publ.
34. But not as increased by sums owed to third parties, see CRvB, 23 February 1993, *RSV* 1993/240.
35. Although a number of restrictions have been attempted as regards "accountability of payments" they have been overruled. See ECJ, 14 July 1998, *JAR* 1998, 229; *cf.* Loesberg E. and Knüppe B.F.M., *Advocatenblad* 1999, pp. 384–385; Schaink P.R.W., *TvI* 1999, p. 92.
36. Noordam F., Inleiding Social-zekerheidsrecht, Deventer, 1998, p. 102.

The financing of pension liabilities is covered to a limited extent.[37] Compensation awards granted by a first-instance canton judge in the context of art. 7:685 BW proceedings for judicial rescission of the employment contract[38] are not guaranteed, and the same applies to sums awarded as compensation in the judicial termination of fixed-term contracts.[39]

The British legislation has manifestly prompted the third variant offered by Article 3 of the Directive.[40] Britain's National Insurance Fund stands guarantor for the payment of:

(a) any arrears of pay in respect of the first eight weeks from the date on which the employer became insolvent;[41]
(b) pay for the statutory notice period;[42]
(c) holiday pay for the last twelve months (up to a maximum of six weeks' pay);
(d) the basic compensation awarded for unfair dismissal;[43]
(e) any statuary severance payments to which the employee is entitled;
(f) the payment of unpaid pension scheme contributions.[44]

It is, however, important to note that in Britain a general ceiling is set for the guarantee of claims for amounts that can be referred to regular periods.[45] All the indications are that, in practical terms, this ceiling greatly reduces the significance of Britain's guarantee institution, since many employees nowadays earn twice the amount set as the ceiling.

In the case of Belgium the legislative arrangements for the guarantee of claims do not tally exactly with any of the three options offered by the Directive, since they are based on the date of company closure. Under Article 2(1) of Sluitingswet '67 the *Sluitingsfonds* stands guarantor for debts for pay, payments and benefits due by virtue of the individual contract of employment or collective agreement as regards:

(a) outstanding pay for a maximum of two months up to a sum of 1860 Euro per month;[46]

---

37. See art. 64(3) WW ; *cf.* CRvB 19 July 1994, WW 1993/40, *RSV* 1995/36; CRvB, 12 May 1998, *Pensioenjurisprudentie* 1998/50.
38. *Cf.* CRvB 27 October 1992, *RSV* 1993/100; *AB* 1993/227.
39. CRvB 2 February 1993, *RSV* 1993/142; CRvB 20 May 1997, *RSV* 1997/230; see Chapter 4, Section 6 below.
40. EC Commission, COM(95)164 final, 15.06.1995, p. 27.
41. See section 184(1)(a) ERA. In Britain section 185 ERA defines a so-called "appropriate date" from which guarantee by the Fund starts to run. This is the point in time when the employer became insolvent or when the employee's employment ended, with the later of the two being the decisive one.
42. See section 184(1)(b) ERA as specified by section 86. More favourable notice periods based on individual contracts of employment or collective agreements are not covered by the Fund's guarantee.
43. See section 84 ERA. This does not, however, include additional compensatory awards: see Chapter 4, Section 3 below; see also Slade E., Tolley's Employment Handbook, Bath, 1966, p. 246 and Selwyn N., Selwyn's Law of Employment, London, 1996, p. 204.
44. See section 124 Pension Schemes Act.
45. See section 186 ERA. As at 1 April 1998 the ceiling was £210 per debt per week. *Cf.* also Harvey, *op. cit.*, Division G No. 39.
46. See art. 7(1)(2) Royal Decree (KB) of 6 July 1967.

(b) the pay of employees who in a bankruptcy situation continue working up to the time of a subsequent transfer;
(c) pay for the notice period, subject to a maximum of 1860 Euro per month;[47]
(d) holiday allowance for white-collar workers, calculated on the basis of pay not exceeding 1860 Euro per month;[48]
(e) compensation in lieu of notice, subject to a maximum of 1860 Euro per month;[49]
(f) other allowances and benefits based on collective agreements,[50] again subject to a maximum of 1860 Euro per month;
(g) supplementary allowances paid to older employees in the context of bridging pensions;
(h) redundancy payments.[51]

Like Britain, Belgium also applies an overall ceiling (amounting to 22500 Euro) for the total claims of any individual employee that are met by the *Sluitingsfonds*.[52]

4. FINANCING AND RECOVERY

In Germany, Belgium and Britain the guarantee institutions are financed by contributions paid exclusively by employers; only in The Netherlands is the scheme funded in equal parts by contributions from both employers and employees.[53]

In cases where the guarantee institution takes over the making of payments, legislative arrangements in the four countries studied differ as regards the manner in which the institution can then recover the sums concerned from bankrupt employers.

In Belgium the rules provide that when the *Sluitingsfonds* makes payments it can then, in its turn, claim them back from the employer. If the payments it has guaranteed relate to employees' pay, the fund acquires the rights of the employees and can invoke the priority right provided for in the first sentence of Article 19(3 bis) of the Hypotheekwet. In the case of payments not relating to pay the Fund can invoke its own priority right as provided for in the last sentence of Article 19(3 bis) of the Hypotheekwet. Since the employee retains his rights against the bankrupt's estate in regard to sums, which are not paid to him by the *Sluitingsfonds*, it can happen that both the employee and the Fund have priority rights. In such cases, in the event of any payment of the

47. See art. 7(1)(1) Royal Decree (KB) of 6 July 1967.
48. See art. 7(1)(4) Royal Decree (KB) of 6 July 1967. The holiday allowance for manual workers is not guaranteed by the *Sluitingsfond*, but will be paid by a special holiday fund.
49. Art. 7(1)(3) Royal Decree (KB) of 6 July 1967.
50. Art. 7(1)(5 and 7) Royal Decree (KB) of 6 July 1967.
51. See Chapter 4, Section 6 below.
52. See penultimate paragraph of art. 7 Royal Decree (KB) of 6 July 1967.
53. Art. 81(3) WW; *cf.* EC Commission, COM(95)164 final, 15.06.1995, pp. 34–39.

claims the available proceeds are distributed proportionally between the two of them.[54]

In The Netherlands the *UWV* acquires the employee's rights if it pays the latter's claim against the employer on the basis of Title IV of the Werkloosheidswet. In recovering payment from the employer the *UWV* is then in the same position as the employee.[55] In so far as the employee had a priority right, in accordance with art. 6:142 BW this priority is transferred unchanged to the *UWV*.

In Britain the Secretary of State for Employment acquires the employee's rights to the extent that the debt is taken over. If any sum can subsequently be recovered from the bankrupt employer, the money is paid into the National Insurance Fund.[56]

In Germany employees' pay claims, which constitute the basis for the payment of *Insolvenzgeld* are transferred to the *Bundesanstalt für Arbeit*.[57]

5. COMPARISON OF THE ROLE OF THE GUARANTEE INSTITUTIONS IN BANKRUPTCY SITUATIONS

It is apparent from what has been said above that the law in The Netherlands, Belgium, Germany and Britain is largely similar in that in all four countries there are guarantee institutions to take over employees' pay claims in insolvency situations. This spreads a safety net beneath the traditional rules of bankruptcy law that all too often leave employees' claims unpaid. Nevertheless, there are in parts the customary differences to be pointed out between the rules governing the guarantee institutions in the four countries.

As regards *temporal limits* on the guarantee provided The Netherlands and Germany, with three months, score better than Britain with its limit of only two months. Belgium also has a limit of two months, but this is not applied to the guarantee of the pay of employees who in a bankruptcy situation continue working until a subsequent transfer of the business. In such circumstances the coverage can therefore extend over a far more lengthy period.

As far as the *scope* of the coverage is concerned it is notable that most of the schemes apply a fairly restricted concept of pay. This includes in every case pay in the strict sense and usually also pay for the notice period, although in Britain and The Netherlands the latter is limited to the statutory notice period. The same is true of holiday-connected payments, except that in Belgium they are excluded in the case of manual workers. On the other hand expense allowances, a thirteenth-month's pay and other benefits deriving from collective agreements, as well as the remittance of pension contributions or

54. Herman J., De werknemer en het faillissement van zijn werkgever, *Oriëntatiegids*, 1983/1, p. 11.
55. See art. 66 WW; *cf.* HR 19 June 1998, *JAR* 1998/169.
56. See section 189 ERA.
57. See §187 SGB III.

the associated financing and the payment of contributions for or benefits from schemes supplementing statutory social security, are named as capable of guarantee by the guarantee institution in only one country. Lastly, the legislative provisions in Belgium and Britain contain precise ceilings for the coverage of employees' pay claims, whereas the provisions in The Netherlands and Germany set no such ceiling. From the point of view of a *ceiling on the amount*, therefore, the schemes in The Netherlands and Germany clearly score much better than those in Belgium and Britain.

All in all, when compared with those in the other countries The Netherlands scheme certainly emerges in a reasonably favourable light. This palls somewhat, of course, when it is remembered that in The Netherlands half of the financing is paid for by employees themselves, whereas in the other countries the costs are borne wholly by employers.

The existence of the guarantee institutions would appear to signify that the weak position of employees' pay claims in bankruptcy situations as described in Chapter 2 above loses much of its unsatisfactory nature. However, this is the case only to a certain extent. As the present chapter shows, in the countries studied limitations are placed on coverage by the guarantee institutions, in terms of time as well as amount and scope. This means that in respect of their pay claims lying outside these limits employees must fall back on their "ordinary" position as creditors in the employer's bankruptcy. In these cases they are again faced with the ranking described in Chapter 2.

The conclusion reached in that chapter that the ranking of employees' pay claims in bankruptcy situations needs to be strengthened also remains relevant for two other reasons. First, the ranking system also determines the relationship between the different post-bankruptcy liabilities or expenses of the estate and consequently affects the position of the pay claims of employees who after the bankruptcy judgment continue working at the estate's expense. Second, a higher ranking is relevant to the guarantee institutions' right of recourse. After making payments to employees the guarantee institutions always acquire the latter's pay claims; hence, the stronger the position of those claims with respect to other creditors, the more recourse the guarantee institutions have to recovery of the money. This reduces the burden on public funds.

4. Protection Against Dismissal in Bankruptcy

1. INTRODUCTION

The bankruptcy of a (legal) person who operates a company is usually accompanied by the dismissal of (some of) its employees. In the case of legal persons bankruptcy leads to a liquidation if the reorganization and restoration of the company to a sound financial footing does not seem feasible within the context of the existing legal person. Unless the employees in the bankrupt's company are still needed for the completion of projects and work in the meantime, they must be dismissed as quickly as possible in order to avoid continuing to burden the estate with pay claims.[1] To what extent is this possible, and what protection do employees have in a situation of this kind?

In the present chapter the following issues are discussed in succession:

- possibilities of dismissal in bankruptcy situations (Section 2);
- judicial control of dismissal to enforce the law in general (Section 3);
- fixed-term contracts and specific bans on dismissal (Section 4);
- notice periods (Section 5);
- compensation for dismissal and redundancy payments (Section 6);
- collective dismissal (Section 7).

In some instances bankruptcy is not used to liquidate the company, and a course is set instead towards a so-called "re-start". In this situation the entire workforce, or part of it, is dismissed but subsequently all or some of the previous employees are taken (back) into employment by the person who is the new employer or transferee. The legal aspects of this situation are not discussed in the present chapter but are dealt with in Chapter 5 below.

With the exception of the role of the German *Betriebsrat*, which for systematic reasons is included in the present chapter, the participation aspects of dismissal in bankruptcy situations are discussed later in Chapter 6.

2. POSSIBILITIES OF DISMISSAL IN BANKRUPTCY SITUATIONS

The first question to arise concerns the consequences of the bankruptcy judgment as regards the continuance of the contracts of employment concluded by employees with the bankrupt employer. Are they perhaps rendered *de jure* null and void by the bankruptcy judgment? If not, to what extent is a receiver absolutely free to dismiss the employees concerned?

1. See art. 40(2) Fw.

R. Blanpain, A.T.J.M. Jacobs (eds.), Employee Rights in Bankruptcy, 23–44.

In Belgium it could, in theory, be contended that a bankruptcy brings into play a precedence within the meaning of Article 26 of the Wet op de Arbeidsovereenkomsten[2] which puts an end to obligations arising from existing contracts of employment. Although as a general rule this is rejected by case-law,[3] it is nevertheless conceivable that in a particular situation one of the circumstances signifies the operation of such precedence and, furthermore, originates in the bankruptcy.[4] In addition, in Belgium Article 46 of the Faillissementswet stipulates that the *curator* (receiver) must decide within a period of 15 days after the bankruptcy judgment whether he wishes to continue the contracts of employment. During this time he is free to decide to terminate the employment relationships,[5] but should he fail to make any decision by the time the 15 day period has expired that omission is deemed *de jure* to be equivalent to termination.[6]

In Britain, in the winding-up procedure the receiver/liquidator is not bound by the existing contracts of employment. The company's business activity ceases, and the appointment of a receiver of this kind also automatically entails the dismissal of its employees. The latter do, of course, have a claim for damages against the company for breach of contract. In the procedure involving an administrative receiver the latter is free to continue (adopt) the contracts of employment although he must make an explicit decision to do so. The law stipulates only that he cannot be taken to have adopted a contract of employment by reason of anything done or omitted to be done within 14 days after his appointment.[7]

In The Netherlands the general presumption in law is that the employer has no freedom to dismiss employees. Under the BBA (Buitengewoon Besluit Arbeidsver-houdingen) an employer who wishes to terminate an employment relationship needs prior authorization to do so from the Center of Work and Income (CWI, formerly the Director of a District Employment Services Authority]. Although the bankruptcy judgment does not *ipso jure* signify the end of the current contracts of employment and equally does not constitute grounds for summary dismissal, the *curator* (receiver) can terminate the contracts of employment without obtaining authorization: he does not have to observe the general prohibition of dismissal.[8] This rule is based on a

---

2. Law of 3 July 1978 concerning Contracts of Employment (*BS*, 22-6-1978).
3. Hof van Cassatie, 24 February 1992, *RW* 1992–93, 157.
4. Rasschaert K., Veys F. and van Hoogenbemt H., in: Faillissement
5. Mergits B., Vanachter O. et al., Aanwerven Tewerkstellen Ontslaan, Antwerp, 1987, pp. 0201–10.
6. Rasschaert K. and Veys F., Nieuwe faillissementswet en wet gerechtelijk akkoord, *Oriëntatiegids*, 1997/11, p. 199.
7. See section 44(2) Insolvency Act 1986; *cf.* Fletcher I.F., The Law of Insolvency, London, 1996, p. 374.
8. Art. 6(2) (c) BBA, brought into force as from 1 January 1989 by virtue of the Law of 1 December 1988, *Stb.* 1988, 573; van den Boom C., Arbeidsovereenkomst Kluwer, Commentaar BBA 1945, Suppl. 178, July 1997, Art. 6–261 and Jacobs A.T.J.M. and Heerma van Voss G.J.J., Elementair sociaal recht, Alphen a/d Rijn, 1996, p. 151. Such authorization had previously been required for years: HR 13 February 1951, *NJ* 1951, 371; *cf.* HR 5 December 1975, *NJ* 1976, 269. See also v. d. Heuvel L.H., Rechten van werknemers bij faillissement, Alphen a/d Rijn, 1981, p. 60.

reconsideration of the conflict between the interests of the employees concerned and those of the bankruptcy creditors. Pay owed as a post-bankruptcy liability or expense of the estate would be too great an amount if the receiver had to follow the BBA procedure.[9] The new Wet Flexibiliteit en Zekerheid[10] has confirmed the non-applicability of the BBA prohibition to bankruptcy situations. Although in accordance with art. 68(2) Fw. receivers in The Netherlands need permission from the examining court to terminate contracts of employment and dismiss employees, this is almost never refused. Since the BBA is not applicable, there is no reason for receivers to terminate the contract of employment by pursuing the route of judicial rescission ex art. 7:685 BW. Although this route is not excluded in bankruptcy situations it is seldom followed in practice, since receivers would thereby invite the imposition of compensation for dismissal.[11]

In Germany an employer whose company has a *Betriebsrat* (works council) is obliged to consult the latter before proceeding with any dismissal. Failure to do so renders the dismissal invalid. If the *Betriebsrat* has objections, it must make them known within one week (within 3 days in the case of summary dismissal). If it lodges a formal objection (*Widerspruch*) and the employee himself also institutes legal proceedings, the latter remains in employment until the legal dispute before the first-instance court has ended.[12]

Just as in The Netherlands, in Germany the bankruptcy judgment does not automatically terminate the contracts of employment and equally does not constitute grounds justifying summary dismissal.[13] In bankruptcy situations a German receiver must also observe this preliminary testing of dismissal, which means that he too must consult the *Betriebsrat*.[14] He must comply with the obligation to provide information in good time and give the *Betriebsrat* a week to state its position. However, if the receiver's decision is to close down the business entirely and he informs the *Betriebsrat* that the entire workforce is being dismissed with the statutory period of notice as laid down in §113(1)(2) InsO on the grounds of company closure, the *Betriebsrat* has no option but to give its agreement. This is because its recourse to *Widerspruch* is confined to several grounds stated restrictively in law.[15]

---

9. Bijl. Hand. TK 19 810, No. 3, p. 2.
10. Law of 14 May 1998, *Stb.* 1998, 300, art. II, under B, art. 6(2)(c) BBA.
11. It is quite conceivable for an employee to have already submitted an application for judicial rescission immediately after the bankruptcy, as a way of being awarded compensation. It can be contended that compensation awarded in this way has the status of a liability or expense of the estate.
12. §102 BetrVG; *cf.* Jacobs A.T.J.M., Inleiding tot het Duitse arbeidsrecht, Arnhem, 1993, p. 114.
13. See BAG 25.10.1968, *NJW* 1969, 1525; *cf.* Müller-Glöge, Erfurter Kommentar zum Arbeitsrecht, Munich, 1998 (hereinafter "EK"), §626 BGB, Rn. 117. Failing special circumstances, only ordinary termination with notice is available to the receiver in bankruptcy situations, not summary dismissal. This can be inferred from §113 InsO, which uses the phrase *ordentliche Kündigung*; *cf.* Duwell J., Kölner Schrift zur Insolvenzordnung, Berlin 1997, p. 1112.
14. Mönning R.-D., Betreibsfortführung in der Insolvenz, Cologne, 1997, p. 212; Müller-Glöge, EK, §113 InsO, Rn. 24.
15. §102(3) BetrVG; *cf.* Duwell J., *op. cit.*, p. 1119.

In cases where, on the other hand, the receiver adopts a *selective* dismissal strategy, under the former legislation the *Betriebsrat* still had a role to play at this stage. The receiver had to take account of the ground for *Widerspruch* stated in §102 BetrVG, viz. total or partial failure on the part of the employer to give due consideration to social factors in selecting employees for dismissal. In accordance with case-law, this ground means that those employees most seriously affected by dismissal should come last on the list. However, the present-day *Insolvenzordnung*, in force as from 1 October 1996/1 January 1999, provides that where a so-called *Interessenausgleich* procedure has been carried out (see Chapter 6, Section 3 below) which contains a list of the names of those employees who are being dismissed for economic business reasons, the basic presumption is that the dismissal of those on the list is legally valid.[16] This has vastly reduced the preliminary testing of dismissals by the *Betriebsrat*.[17]

In short, in cases of the dismissal of the entire workforce the German receiver is in practice as free as his colleagues in Belgium, Britain and The Netherlands, but as regards selective dismissal his options are somewhat more restricted although no longer so much as in the past.

3. JUDICIAL CONTROL OF DISMISSALS IN GENERAL

In Germany an employee whose employment has been terminated by the receiver has the option, on the basis of the principle that normal dismissals law applies in bankruptcy situations,[18] of contesting his dismissal before the *Arbeitsgericht* as not being "socially justified".[19] However, in the event of a total company closure the receiver has little to fear from judicial intervention since these circumstances unquestionably constitute "urgent operational reasons" within the meaning of §1(1)KSchG, which means that the dismissal is deemed "socially justified".[20] Furthermore the receiver is able – despite a ban on dismissal by reason of a business transfer (see Chapter 5 below) – to dismiss some of the employees in the meantime in order to make the rest of the company more saleable at a later date (so-called *vorgezogene betriebsbedingte Kündigung*).[21] In that case, however, under the old legislation he had to follow the procedure of "weighing up the social consequences" which must normally be carried out when reducing the workforce,[22] using the employees' length of

16. §125 InsO; *cf.* Strothmann Y. and Rendels D., Doelen en problemen van de Duitse Insolventiewet, *TvI*, 1998/7, p. 156.
17. The implications also apply where the conduct of the *Interessenausgleich* does not include all the aspects captured in the course of preliminary testing, such as notice periods and bans on dismissal; see in this connection Duwell J., *op. cit.*, p. 1120.
18. Strothmann Y. and Rendels D., *loc. cit.*, p. 156.
19. See §1 KSchG. Only in §113(2) InsO has it been stipulated that this application must always be made to the court within a period of three weeks, whereas in other cases a longer period had sometimes been allowed; see Preis, EK, §613a BGB, Rn.122.
20. §1(1) KSchG; see LAG Hamm 9.4.1980, *ZIP* 1980, 470.
21. *Cf.* BAG 26.5.1983, *AP* No. 34 regarding §613 BGB.
22. §1(3) KSchG; *cf.* BAG 16.9.1982, *AP* No. 4 regarding §22 KO.

service, age and possible number of dependants as criteria. But this was not appropriate, since in normal "selective dismissal" in Germany even more *soziale Gesichtspunkte* apply, one of them being the vague rule that those employees most seriously affected by dismissal should come last on the list. It proved difficult in practice, with the application of this "weighing up the social consequences", for the receiver to make a viable choice between employees that would also be subsequently accepted by the court.[23] Consequently, since 1 October 1996/1 January 1999 in the new legislation it has been made somewhat simpler for the receiver to dismiss employees selectively.

When in a bankruptcy situation a so-called *Interessenausgleich* has been agreed between the receiver and the *Betriebsrat* (see Chapter 6, Section 3 below) containing a list of the names of those employees who are being dismissed for operational reasons, there is a presumption that the dismissal is "socially justified".[24] The court will then apply only three criteria (length of service, age and number of dependants) in testing whether the selection has been made incorrectly – which on the basis of §125(1)(2) InsO is out of the question if an *ausgewogene Personalstruktur* (balanced workforce) has been preserved or created.

If the company has no *Betriebsrat* or if after three weeks' negotiations an *Interessenausgleich* has still not been agreed, under §126 InsO the receiver can request the *Arbeitsgericht* nevertheless to allow the major changes to the company and to pronounce that dismissal for operational reasons is "socially justified". Here again, in its testing the court applies only the criteria of the employees' length of service, age and number of dependants.[25] This pronouncement by the *Arbeitsgericht* is also binding in subsequent dismissal procedures unless the situation has changed fundamentally after the court hearing (e.g. as a result of a change of ownership of the company). In accordance with §126(2) InsO this relaxation of dismissals law also applies in the event of transfer of the business by reason of bankruptcy and to some extent broadens the possibility of transferring a company in a slimmed-down form.

In Britain, in accordance with section 94 ERA an employee with more than one year length of service cannot be dismissed unfairly by his employer. The concept of unfair dismissal is deemed to cover, in particular, dismissal contrary to law which cannot be justified by the conduct of the employee, lack of capability or qualifications on the part of the employee to perform work of the kind that he was employed to do, or redundancy.[26] Under section 111(2) ERA an employee who considers himself to have been unfairly dismissed can present a complaint to that effect to an employment tribunal within a period of three months after his dismissal. If the tribunal finds the complaint to be well-

23. Duwell J., *op. cit.*, p. 1121.
24. This concerns a rebuttable presumption, with the burden of proof reversed and placed on the employee; see Ascheid, EK, §126 InsO, Rn. 6.
25. Kania T., Arbeitsrecht in Konkurs und Insolvenz, *DStR*, 1996/21, p. 835; Mönning R.-D., *op. cit.*, p. 213.
26. See section 98(2) ERA; *cf.* Jefferson M., Principles of Employment Law, London, 1997, p. 245.

founded, the employer can be ordered to reinstate the employee or to pay him compensation.[27] Under section 118 ERA this compensation consists of a basic award plus a compensatory award. The basic award is equal to the amount of the redundancy payment (see Section 6 of the present chapter), while the compensatory award is whatever amount the tribunal considers just and equitable in the circumstances.

These rules are also applicable in principle to dismissal by (administrative) receivers. Since in Britain the redundancy of staff is a given factor in bankruptcy procedures, in this situation there is virtually never any question of unfair dismissal.

In The Netherlands art. 7:681 BW provides for an ex post testing of a dismissal because of *kennelijke onredelijkheid* (manifest unfairness). Normally, little use is made of this form of judicial control since any dismissal will have already been subjected to preliminary testing as to its reasonableness by the CWI. However, the fact that authorization from the CWI does not need to be obtained for dismissal in a bankruptcy situation means that the art. 7:681 BW "manifest unfairness test" would appear to assume independent significance. Also, in case-law there is a basic assumption that a dismissal by the receiver is not in principle exempted from such testing.[28] Admittedly, the specific circumstances of bankruptcy usually mean that the court will rarely be able to deny the economic grounds for dismissals.[29] But the court can still examine whether all the procedural rules for dismissal have been followed, whether the bans on discriminatory dismissal have been observed or – as regards further possible selection – the seniority rule has been complied with, and so on.[30] The question of compensation for dismissal can also arise here, but that aspect is dealt with later in section 6 of the present chapter. Although a receiver in The Netherlands therefore has to reckon with judicial control, such instances would appear to be almost unknown in practice.

In Belgium there is provision under art. 63 WAo for ex post judicial control in relation to the dismissal of manual workers where such dismissal is *willekeurig* (unfair). This possibility also exists in the case of white-collar workers when there is a question of *misbruik van recht* (improper exercise of a right) by the employer. In theory the receiver also has to reckon with these possibilities, but in practice no such cases seem to occur.

27. See sections 113–132 ERA; *cf.* Kay P. and Carr C., Employment Law, London, 1997, p. 140.
28. HR 12 January 1990, *NJ* 1990, 663 (Van Gelder Papier); *cf.* Loesberg E., in: A.M Luttmer-Kat (ed.), Werknemers en insolventie van de werkgever: is de balans in evenwicht?, Insolad Jaarboek 1999, Deventer, 2000, p. 19.
29. Rechtbank Arnhem 11 November 1991, *NJ* 1992, 337.
30. Loesberg E., De werknemer en zijn insolvente werkgever (I), *TvI*, 1998/4, p. 73; Bloemarts J.C.M.G., in: A.M. Luttmer-Kat (ed.), *op. cit.*, p. 78.

4. FIXED-TERM CONTRACTS AND SPECIFIC BANS ON DISMISSAL

A special problem could arise in bankruptcy situations as regards the termination of fixed-term contracts of employment. Given that such contracts are not subject to ordinary termination with notice prior to their date of expiry, is the receiver nevertheless authorized to terminate them? This appears to be the case in all four of the countries studied. In Britain the (administrative) receiver is not bound by existing contracts of employment, while in the other countries the law has invested the receiver with the authority to terminate contracts of employment irrespective of whether they have been concluded for a fixed term or for a period of unspecified duration.[31] Although in Germany employees are entitled under §113(1)(3) InsO to apply for compensation for premature termination of their employment relationship, this gives them only an ordinary claim in bankruptcy.

An enhanced degree of protection against dismissal on particular grounds, for particular groups or in particular situations exists in all four countries. This can be said to apply in general in the event of pregnancy and childbirth and it applies on employee representatives. In addition, each country provides specific protection on the basis of anti-discrimination legislation. The question arises of the extent to which the receiver has to take such specific rules on protection against dismissal into account.

In The Netherlands there is provision for a number of specific bans on dismissal, most of which have since 1 January 1999 been incorporated into the Burgerlijk Wetboek (BW), with one still in force under the legislation on equal treatment for men and women (Awgb: Algemene wet Gelijke Behandeling). By virtue of these bans the employer may not terminate the contract of employment, on pain of the dismissal being ruled null and void, during:

- the first two years of incapacity for work through illness;[32]
- pregnancy and up to six weeks after post-confinement maternity leave;[33]
- military service or alternative compulsory service;[34]
- membership of a works council or permanent committee, etc.[35]

Termination is also prohibited where it involves or is imposed because of:

- discrimination based on race, ethnic origin, religion or sexual orientation;[36]
- a complaint lodged by an employee of contravention of the law on equal treatment for men and women;[37]

31. In the case of Germany: §113 InsO; *cf.* Müller-Glöge,EK, §113 InsO, Rn. 11. In the case of The Netherlands: art. 40 Fw.; see de Wolff D., De arbeidsovereenkomst voor bepaalde tijd, Deventer, 1999, pp. 155–156. In the case of Belgium: art. 46 Fw.
32. Art. 7:670(1) BW.
33. Art. 7:670(2) BW.
34. Art. 7:670(3) BW.
35. Art. 7:670(4) BW.
36. Art. 5(1)(b) Awgb.
37. Arts. 7:646 *et seq.* BW.

- membership of and activities performed on behalf of a trade union;[38]
- attendance at meetings of political organizations to which the employee belongs;[39]
- exercise of the right to parental leave[40] and the right to request an adaptation of working time,[41]
- a business transfer.[42]

For a long time The Netherlands legislation was far from clear as regards the applicability of these specific bans on dismissal to bankruptcy situations.

Since 1 January 1999 the law states that all these bans with the sole exception of that during maternity leave (i.e. pregnancy and post-confinement leave)[43] do not apply "in the event of *beëindiging van de werkzaamheden* [cessation of the work activities] of the company or a part thereof". This is generally the case in bankruptcy situations. Sometimes, however, work activities are continued during bankruptcy and/or the receiver wishes to carry out only selective dismissals, and in these circumstances the *beëindiging van de werkzaamheden* formula does not make matters clear.

Therefore, it is now clearly established that specific bans on dismissal (save that applying during maternity leave) do not preclude dismissal of the entire workforce by the receiver. Their effect in regard to selective dismissal by the receiver remained unclear, however.[44] The bans deriving from anti-discrimination legislation appear to remain fully applicable.

In Belgium the Wet op de Arbeidsovereenkomsten (WAo) contains a number of bans on dismissal that must be observed by the employer.

During the probationary period, failing the existence of just cause recognized by the courts the contract of employment cannot be terminated unilaterally by the employer for a period of at least seven days in the case of manual workers and one month in that of white-collar workers.[45] This also applies in bankruptcy situations.

In addition the contract cannot be terminated by reason of:[46]

- military service and alternative service for conscientious objectors;[47]
- pregnancy;[48]
- a complaint or legal action based on equal treatment for men and women.[49]

In the event of bankruptcy, however, these latter bans on dismissal are not applicable and the employees concerned cease to have any protection. In

38. Art. 7:670(5) BW.
39. Art. 7:670(6) BW.
40. Art. 7:670(7) BW.
41. Art. 3 Wet Aanpassing Arbeidsduur
42. Art. 7:670 BW
43. See art. 7:670b(2) BW, introduced under the Law of 14 May 1998 amending the BW, the BBA (1945) and several other laws (Wet Flexibiliteit en Zekerheid), *Stb.* 1998, 300.
44. See Broekman M.F.H., De ondernemingsraad en faillissement, *ArbeidsRecht* 1999/4, p. 8.
45. See art. 48§4(1) WAo and art. 81§1 WAo respectively.
46. van Eeckhoute W., Sociaal compendium arbeidsrecht 1997–98, Diegem, 1998, p. 1351.
47. Art. 38 §3 WAo.
48. Art. 40 Arbeidswet, Law of 16 March 1971 (*BS*, 30–3–1971).
49. Art. 136 Law of 4 August 1978, *BS*, 17–8–1978.

such a situation grounds exist which are totally unconnected with, for example, the employee's pregnancy.

Lastly, the Belgian legislation provides protection for employee representatives on the works council and workplace health and safety committee[50] and also members of the union delegation.[51] Such representatives can be dismissed only in circumstances where there is just cause or reasons of an economic or technical nature.[52] These grounds for dismissal have to be approved in advance by the relevant sectoral joint committee or, in the absence of such a committee, by the Nationale Arbeidsraad. In the event of the company's bankruptcy the receiver remains under an obligation to observe this consultation procedure.[53] The sole exception is where a judicial decision is issued by the Rechtbank van Koophandel to close down the company's business activities, which automatically signifies the immediate dismissal, or imminent dismissal, of all the employees.[54] Total cessation of the company's business activities clearly precludes any discriminatory treatment of protected employees.

Germany likewise has special forms of legislative protection for particular groups of employees (*besonders geschutzte Arbeitnehmergruppen*) for whom bans on dismissal apply. Apart from a ban on dismissal during military service, the contract of employment cannot be terminated:

- during pregnancy and up to four-months after confinement.[55] This rule is also applicable in bankruptcy situations, which means that for such employees the receiver has to comply with the normal statutory dismissals procedure.[56] However, if he decides on complete company closure this protection against dismissal lapses;
- in the case of disabled employees: those with at least 50% capacity to work and a length of service of at least six months can be dismissed only with the prior consent of the *Integrationsambt*, a body with special responsibility for the welfare of the disabled.[57] This procedure used to remain applicable in principle in bankruptcy situations and had to be observed by the receiver.[58] However, the introduction of the new *Insolvenzordnung* has brought with it the inclusion of a provision which makes the receiver's task easier without prejudicing the interests of disabled employees;[59]

50. Law of 19 March 1991 containing special rules on dismissal for employee representatives on works councils and workplace health and safety committees and for those standing as candidates for election as such (*BS*, 29–3–1991).
51. Nationale Arbeidsraad Collective Agreement No. 5 of 24 May 1971 (*BS*, 1–7–1971). This is a framework agreement which has to be supplemented in detail for each sector or company.
52. Rasschaert K. and Veys F., *loc. cit.*, p. 200; Rasschaert K. et al., *op. cit.*, pp. 246–248; Smeds P., Drie jaar toepassing van de Bijzondere Ontslagregelingswet van 19 maart 1991 deel 2: Ontslag om economische of technische redenen, *Oriëntatiegids*, 1994/6 and 7, p. 142.
53. See the Koninklijk Besluit of 21 May 1991 (*BS*, 28–5–1991).
54. Hof van Cassatie 14 March 1994, *JTT*, 1994, 285.
55. §9(1) MuSchG of 18.4.1968 (*BGBL*. S. 2911).
56. Schlachter, EK, §9 MuSchG, Rn. 6.
57. §§2/85–92/153 SGB IX; formerly §19 SchwbG of 26.8.1986 (*BGBL*. IS. 421, rep. S. 1550).
58. BVerwG 2.7.1991, *AP* No. 1 regarding §21 SchwbG 1986.
59. §89 (3) SGB III; formerly §19(3) SchwbG; *cf.* Steinmeyer,EK, §19 SchwbG Rn. 7.

- in the case of works council members (*Betriebsratmitglieder*) and other employee representatives during their membership of such bodies and for a period of one year after their term if office ends;[60]
- by reason of a business transfer.[61]

In the case of Britain, lastly, although there are no outright bans on dismissal for particular groups/reasons, in certain situations any dismissal is automatically classed as unfair dismissal with all its attendant consequences.[62] This is so in the case of:

- dismissal by reason of or in connection with pregnancy;[63]
- dismissal on grounds of membership or non-membership of a trade union;[64]
- dismissal by reason of the employee's assertion of a statutory right.[65]

However, the significance of these provisions is limited in bankruptcy situations. If the entire workforce is being dismissed owing to a company closure, these exceptions play no part because the employees affected are classed as redundant.[66] It is only in contexts where part of the workforce is being dismissed that there is opportunity for the employee to prove that his situation constitutes unfair dismissal on the grounds of the applicability of the above-mentioned exceptions. If only some of the employees are being dismissed redundancy has no effect in excluding the application of these exceptions.[67] If a complaint of unfair dismissal in bankruptcy situations is successful, payment of the basic award granted to the employee by way of compensation is guaranteed by the National Insurance Fund (see Section 3 above).

5. NOTICE PERIODS

In considering the question of notice periods in bankruptcy situations there is a distinction to be made between those which must be observed by the employer/receiver and those with which the employees must comply. Given the starting-points of the present study, our interest here is confined to the notice periods which must be observed by the receiver.

60. §15 KSchG. However, in accordance with §15(3–4) KSchG they can be dismissed, including by the receiver, in the event of total or partial company closure; *cf.* Duwell J., *op. cit.*, p. 1124; Mönning R.-D., *op. cit.*, p. 211; Müller-Glöge, EK, §113 InsO, Rn. 22–27.
61. §613a(4) BGB. Although this ban also applies to the receiver (*cf.* BAG 26.5.1983, *AP* No. 34 regarding §613a BGB), in practice he is able to circumvent it via the doctrine of *vorgezogene betriebsbedingte Kündigung* (see the preceding Section 3 of this chapter).
62. Hepple B. et al., Employment Security, Leuven, 1994, p. 165 and Lockton J., Employment Law, London, 1996, p. 221.
63. See section 99 ERA.
64. See section 152 TULR(C)A 1992.
65. See section 104 ERA.
66. Lockton J., *op. cit.*, p. 153.
67. See section 105 ERA; *cf.* Kay P. and Carr C., *op. cit.*, p. 145.

Before each of the systems is discussed separately it may be noted that a striking difference is to be observed between Belgium and Britain (and, until recently, Germany) on the one hand, and on the other The Netherlands and, henceforth, Germany. In Belgium and Britain dismissal during bankruptcy is subject to the normal periods of notice: the receiver must observe those stipulated for the employer. In The Netherlands and, nowadays, Germany, although the normal periods of notice also apply in principle they are limited in a great many cases to a maximum that is stipulated specifically for the bankruptcy situation, which means that these periods are in reality greatly shortened.

In Belgium, where the receiver must observe both the relevant statutory notice periods and those stipulated by the contract of employment or collective agreement, the following system applies:

For *manual workers* the statutory period of notice is set at four weeks.[68] This period is doubled in the case of manual workers with at least 20 years' continuous length of service with the same employer. In the case of manual workers with less than six months' continuous length of service a shorter period of notice can be stipulated by collective agreement or individual contract of employment, but always subject to a minimum of one week.[69]

For *white-collar workers* the length of the period of notice differs according to their length of service and annual gross pay:

- for those with annual pay not exceeding 16,250 Euro ("lower-grade white-collar workers"): at least three months, extended by three months for each five-year period of service with the employer concerned;[70]
- for those with annual pay exceeding 16,250 Euro ("higher-grade white-collar workers"): the period of notice is fixed by mutual agreement, with length of service taken into account.[71] A kind of standard formula is widely used for calculating this period: the "Claeys" formula, compiled by legal scholars on the basis of existing court decisions.[72]

The length of the notice period for higher-ranking white-collar workers may not be determined by collective agreement.[73]

Likewise in Britain, dismissal during bankruptcy is subject to the normal system of statutory notice periods.[74] These are determined by the employee's continuous length of service with the employer concerned:[75]

- for employees with less than two years' length of service the minimum period of notice is one week;

68. Art. 59 WAo.
69. Art. 60 WAo.
70. Art. 82§2 WAo.
71. Art. 82§3 WAo.
72. Humblet and Rigaux, Algemene beginselen van Belgisch arbeidsrecht, Diegen, 1997, p. 177.
73. Hof van Cassatie 16 March 1987, *JTT*, 1987, 441.
74. See section 86 ERA. With the exception of summary dismissal, which is usually possible only on the grounds of personal misconduct on the part of the employee and not for economic reasons (see section 86(6) ERA).
75. Jefferson M., *op. cit.*, p. 189.

- for employees with two years' length of service or more the minimum period of notice is one week for each year of employment with the employer concerned, subject to a maximum of 12 weeks.

Notice periods longer than these statutory periods are frequently stipulated in Britain in the contract of employment itself or by collective agreement, but (administrative) receivers are not bound by them.[76]

In The Netherlands, in principle the receiver must also observe the notice periods stipulated for dismissal by the employer.[77] However, in accordance with art. 40 Fw. the maximum notice period that has to be observed by the receiver is limited to six weeks, regardless of whether a longer period has been prescribed by law or collective agreement (art. 40(1) Fw.).[78] As long ago as 1988 the SER urged that the limit should be removed,[79] but so far nothing has come of this.

Up till 1 January 1999 a lengthening of this maximum was in force for the benefit of employees in the 45–65 age group, whereby the notice period could be lengthened by up to an additional 13 weeks to a maximum of 19 weeks in bankruptcy situations.[80] As from 1 January 1999 this provision has been abolished,[81] but will in the meantime continue to take effect for employees who on that date were already aged 45 or over, so long as it is not altered by employers.[82]

The rule already in force before 1 January 1999 whereby the system of the *aanzegdag*[83] never results in the lengthening of the notice period in bankruptcy situations has remained unchanged.[84]

In Germany, until recently the receiver who decided to terminate the contract of employment had to observe the normal statutory notice periods.[85] These are set on a rising scale based on the employee's length of service, reaching a maximum of seven months after 20 years' continuous length of service.[86] The introduction of the *Insolvenzordnung* has brought, as from 1 October 1996/1 January 1999, a separate rule applying to bankruptcy

---

76. Lockton J., *op. cit.*, p. 162.
77. Bloemarts J.C.M.G., De positie van werknemers en hun vertegenwoordigers bij faillissement en surséance van betaling, *Sociaal recht*, 1998/6, p. 180 and Fase W.J.P.M., Inleiding sociaal recht, Groningen, 1987, p. 44.
78. Polak N.J. and Polak C.E., Faillissementsrecht, Deventer, 1999, p. 89 and Jacobs A.T.J.M. and Heerma van Voss G.J.J., *op. cit.*, p. 161.
79. Opinion issued on the reform of dismissals law (*Advies herziening ontslagrecht*), 16 September 1988.
80. See art. 40(3) (former) Fw. subst. art. 7:672(2) (former) BW; *cf.* Zakboek Arbeidsrecht (2), Individueel arbeidsrecht, Suppl. 46 (June 1996), Title B. 4–3.6, p. 21; Polak N.J. and Polak C.E., Faillissementsrecht, Alphen a/d Rijn, 1997, p. 95; Oosthout H.B., De doorstart van een insolvente onderneming, Deventer, 1998, p. 86.
81. Law of 14 May 1998, *Stb.* 1998, 300.
82. Luttmer-Kat A.M., in: A.M. Luttmer-Kat (ed.), *op. cit.*, p. 6.
83. The *aanzegdag* is the date on which the employment relationship is terminated and from which the notice period starts to run. Failing any written agreement or custom or practice stipulating otherwise, it is defined as the end of a calendar month (see art. 7:672(1) BW).
84. HR 22 May 1970, *NJ* 1970, 419.
85. See §22 KO. This meant that the receiver was able to ignore longer notice periods laid down by collective agreements or in individual contracts of employment.
86. See §622(2)(7) BGB; *cf.* Jacobs A.T.J.M., *op. cit.*, p. 127.

situations under §113(1)(2) InsO. This sets a maximum notice period of three months in so far as no shorter period is applicable by virtue of law or collective agreement.[87] The employee can, however, present an ordinary claim for compensation in the bankruptcy procedure based on the shortening of the normal period of notice.[88]

To illustrate the findings of the present section, a summary is given below of the periods of notice which at present must be observed by the receiver in a bankruptcy situation in the four countries studied for, by way of example, an employee aged 55 with a continuous length of service of 20 years:

Belgium:	a minimum of eight weeks for manual workers and 72 weeks for white-collar workers;
Britain:	12 weeks;
The Netherlands:	a maximum of six weeks (16 weeks where transitional law is applicable);
Germany:	a maximum of 13 weeks.

6 COMPENSATION FOR DISMISSAL AND REDUNDANCY PAYMENTS

The past few years have witnessed a growing trend in European countries for it to become customary for the employer, in making dismissals, to be required not only to observe a period of notice but also to make certain forms of payment to the employees affected. In the four countries studied here this can come about in relation to a particular company closure on a relatively *ad hoc* basis by way of individual contracts or collectively agreed provisions ("social plans"). But a more general form of regulation also exists. In Britain this is provided for by statute, in Belgium by legislation and by collective agreements that are decreed generally applicable, and in The Netherlands and Germany by collective agreements plain and simple. The question arises as to how far the receiver in bankruptcy situations is also bound by the rules in question.

In Britain an employee who is dismissed by reason of *redundancy*[89] has the right to a redundancy payment on the basis of the Employment Rights Act 1996 (ERA). The amount of this payment varies according to the employee's age, length of service with the employer concerned and weekly pay and by virtue of section 162 ERA is calculated as follows:

- for employees aged 18–21, half a week's pay for each year of employment;
- for employees aged 22–40, one week's pay for each year of employment;

87. Kania T., *loc. cit.*, p. 834 and Duwell J., *op. cit.*, p. 1113; Preis E.K., §613a BGB, Rn. 121.
88. *Cf.* BAG 6.12.1984, *AP* No. 14 regarding §61 KO; see Preis,E.K., §613a BGB, Rn. 122; Möller-Glöge, EK, §113 InsO, Rn. 31–34.
89. Redundancy is defined in section 139 ERA as dismissal attributable to (a) the fact that the business has ceased to exist or (b) the fact that the requirements of the business for work of the kind performed by the employee have ceased or diminished.

- for employees aged 41–65, one and a half week's pay for each year of employment.

This calculation is based on a maximum weekly pay of £210, with only the last 20 years of employment being taken into account. The maximum sum that must be paid therefore amounts to £6300.[90] The same amount is payable in bankruptcy situations.[91]

In Belgium in the event of company closure an employee has a statutory right to a payment called a *sluitingspremie* on the basis of the Sluitingswet '66. Closure is defined as the definitive cessation of the main activity of the company or of a part thereof where the number of employees is reduced to less than a quarter of the average number employed. This payment is due from the employer, but in the event of his inability to pay is guaranteed by the *Sluitingsfonds*.[92]

Eligibility for this *sluitingspremie* (compensation for dismissal in the event of closure) is confined to employees:

- of companies employing at least 20 employees on average during the past calendar year, who
- have at least one year's length of service with the employer concerned;
- are employed under an employment contract of unspecified duration;
- are not being (summarily) dismissed for just cause;
- are being dismissed either at the time of the closure or during the 12 months (18 months in the case of white-collar workers) preceding the closure or the 12 months following the closure.[93]

The amount of the payment is 113 Euro for each year of employment with the employer concerned plus, for older employees, an additional 113 Euro for each year of age over 45,[94] subject in both cases to an upper limit of 20 years to be taken into account. Receipt of compensation in lieu of notice or unemployment benefit does not preclude entitlement to the *sluitingspremie*.

In bankruptcy situations, employees who meet the stipulated criteria are entitled to the *sluitingspremie* provided the business concerned is actually closed down.[95] However, if the receiver continues to operate the business no such entitlement exists,[96] although in cases involving a partial closure meeting the criteria stipulated in art. 2 Sluitingswet '66 those employees who are dismissed are deemed eligible for such a payment.

---

90. One and a half weeks' maximum weekly pay of £210 multiplied by twenty; *cf.* Kay P. and Carr C., *op. cit.*, p. 165.
91. See section 386 Insolvency Act 1986.
92. See art. 4(6) Sluitingswet '66.
93. See arts. 1 and 4(1–5) Sluitingswet '66.
94. See art. 6 Sluitingswet '66.
95. Arbeidshof Brussels 10 January 1985, *Soc. Kron.*, 1983, 418.
96. Arbeidshof Liège 7 June 1985, *JTT*, 1985, 359 and Arbeidshof Leuven 1 April 1982, *Soc. Kron.*, 1983, 418.

Also, in collective dismissal situations Belgian employees are entitled to a special form of compensation provided under a generally applicable collective agreement.[97] This compensation, which in accordance with Title IV of Collective Agreement No. 10 is payable for a period of four months, is equal to half of the difference between the net reference wage and the unemployment benefits that the employee is able to claim.[98] Thus, it is an additional payment on top of the unemployment benefit to which the employees are entitled and cannot be cumulated with the above-mentioned compensation for company closure.[99] In a bankruptcy where a *sluitingspremie* is paid employees who are dismissed have no right, for this reason, to the special compensation provided for under Collective Agreement No. 10.

In The Netherlands no general statutory right exists to any form of compensation for dismissal. A first-instance Canton Court does usually award compensation in cases where it – other than on the grounds of a *dringende reden* [substantial reason] – decides on judicial rescission of the contract of employment (art. 7:685 BW) or reaches the conclusion that the dismissal was *kennelijk onredelijk* [manifestly unfair] (art. 7:681 BW). In assessing the amount of such compensation the court applies the following basic rule:

- one month's pay for each year of service under the age of 40;
- one and a half months' pay for each year of service between the ages of 40 and 50;
- two months' pay for each year of service over the age of 50.

However, these amounts may be increased or reduced in the light of the circumstances of a particular case (primarily the degree of culpability of the dismissal).

In addition, the right to compensation for dismissal is frequently stipulated by the individual contract of employment or provided for in a collective agreement or a *sociaal plan*.[100] In such cases the compensation can take the form of a lump-sum severance payment and/or supplementation of a statutory benefit.

97. Nationale Arbeidsraad Collective Agreement No. 10 of 8 May 1973 concerning collective dismissal, decreed generally applicable by Royal Decree of 6 August 1973 (*BS*, 17–8–1973); *cf* Blanpain R. and Vanachter O., Schets van het Belgische arbeidsrecht, Bruges, 1997, p. 241. The definition of the concept of collective dismissal in Collective Agreement No. 10 is the same as that in Nationale Arbeidsraad Collective Agreement No. 24; see Rauws W. et al., Schuldeisers en ondernemingen in moeilijkheden, Kalmthout, 1994, p. 169.

98. This compensation likewise may possibly be paid by the Sluitingsfonds in its capacity as a guarantee institution, which can then claim it back from the employer or his bankrupt estate.

99. See art. 6 Nationale Arbeidsraad Collective Agreement No. 10.

100. A *sociaal plan* is a kind of redundancy programme regulating the labour-relations consequences of a workforce reduction, such as the criteria to be applied in selecting employees for dismissal, forms of compensation and the right to be offered suitable alternative work; see van Slooten J., De aard en werking van het sociaal plan, *Sociaal recht*, 1995/12, p. 362 and Oosthout H.B., *op. cit.*, p. 85. When concluded with a trade union, it may have the status of a collective agreement: see HR 20 March 1998, *JAR* 1998/127; HR 26 May 2000, *JAR* 2000/151.

In bankruptcy situations the receiver can circumvent the payment of compensation for dismissal simply by dismissing the employees on the basis of art. 40 Fw and thereby sidestepping proceedings before the Canton Court. This strategy does not, in itself, make it impossible for employees to institute legal proceedings against the receiver on the grounds of *kennelijk onredelijk ontslag* [unfair dismissal] as a way of obtaining compensation. Their chances of success in doing so must not be overestimated, because a dismissal carried out by the receiver is not readily deemed to constitute unfair dismissal. Furthermore, in such cases the interests of the employees concerned have to be weighed not so much against those of the employer (receiver) as against those of all the other creditors.[101] Should the court, nevertheless, reach the conclusion that the dismissal by the receiver was unfair, the debt in question is ranked as a *boedelschuld* (post-bankruptcy liability or expense of the estate) with the concomitant high priority for employees dismissed unfairly by the receiver.[102] However, the situation is different as regards compensation for dismissal which is provided for in an individual contract of employment, collective agreement or *sociaal plan*; in the event of dismissal by the receiver such compensation is not classed as a liability or expense of the estate, nor is it capable of being proved.[103] Claims deriving from this kind of arrangement for compensation are capable of being proved and classed as preferential claims only in cases where dismissal had been carried out by the employer before he was adjudged bankrupt.[104] The same applies to claims for compensation deriving from termination of the employment relationship which was agreed before the date of bankruptcy but pre-empted by the fact of the bankruptcy judgment.[105]

There is no known case-law on the status in bankruptcy situations of compensation awarded as part of judicial rescission of the contract of employment by a Canton Court ex art. 7:685 BW. The receiver will of course never take the art. 7:685 BW line, but an employee could well decide to do so just to obtain compensation. In the literature it is argued that compensation awards of this kind must be classed as *boedelschulden* [liabilities or expenses of the estate] provided that the court has issued the rescission order before the notice period has expired.[106]

Case-law does exist as regards whether compensation awarded as part of judicial rescission ex art. 7:685 BW is covered by the guarantee scheme in the Werkloosheidswet (WW). Up until now claims based on compensation awards deriving from judicial rescission were rejected by the bodies, which administer

---

101. Bloemarts J.C.M.G., *loc. cit.*, *Sociaal Recht*, 1988/6, p. 181.
102. HR 12 January 1990, *NJ* 1990, 662 (Van Gelder Papier); Loesberg E., in: A.M. Luttmer-Kat (ed.), *op.cit.*, p. 19.
103. *Cf.* Hof den Bosch 7 March 1988, *NJ* 1990 and HR 12 January 1990, *NJ* 1990, 662. Although it is possible that the bankrupt or the creditors will hold the receiver personally liable for carrying out unlawful dismissal.
104. HR 23 May 1980, *NJ* 1980, 502.
105. *Cf.* Rechtbank Amsterdam 23 December 1998 and Hof Amsterdam 3 February 2000 (X vs Fokker receivers); discussed by Jacobs A.T.J.M. and Vriesendorp R.D. in *TvI* 2000 (Fokkerspecial), pp. 40–42.
106. Loesberg E. and Grapperhaus F.B.J., in: A.M. Luttmer-Kat (ed.), *op. cit.*, pp. 23 and 70.

the guarantee scheme. And this policy has been endorsed by the Centrale Raad van Beroep [Central Appeal Tribunal].[107]

In Germany, as in The Netherlands, there is no statutory right to compensation for dismissal. Many dismissals do, however, take place in the context of the statutory provisions on a *Sozialplan* ["social plan", i.e. special redundancy programme] whereby the employees affected are granted specified forms of compensation. Under the old *Konkursordnung* the status of the *Sozialplan* in bankruptcy had been challenged in court and temporarily regulated by the Sozialplangesetz .[108] This arrangement has been retained only partially in the new *Insolvenzordnung*.

Under the actual law a distinction must be made between "social plans" which are agreed on after the bankruptcy and "social plans" agreed before the bankruptcy. "Social plans" which are agreed on after the bankruptcy, give rise, on the basis of §123(2) InsO, to post-bankruptcy debts (*Masseverbindlichkeiten)*, which means that such claims stand a good chance of being met. But only to a maximum of two and a half months' pay (broadly defined) per employee for such a compensation. In addition such claims cannot, in all, amount to more than one third of the total bankruptcy debts.[109] "Social plans" dating from three months at the latest before the bankruptcy judgment may be terminated both by the receiver and by the *Betriebsrat*. The employees involved can then be included in the *Sozialplan* ex §123 InsO (§124 InsO). Employees' claims based on old "social plans" that have not been terminated are classed as ordinary pre-bankruptcy claims.[110]

7. COLLECTIVE DISMISSAL

In 1975 the EC Council adopted a Directive relating to collective redundancies.[111] The Directive was amended in 1992[112] and consolidated in 1998.[113] The Directive contains provisions regulating the notification of, provision of information to and consultation of employee representatives and the competent public authority, in good time, in the event of projected dismissals on a certain scale. Furthermore, any such collective dismissals cannot take effect until a period of 30 days has elapsed after notification, in order to allow time for compliance with the various requirements to be feasible in practice. The fact that the Directive has since been implemented by all four of the countries studied here, i.e. The Netherlands, Belgium, Germany and

107. CRvB 27 October 1992, *RSV* 1993/100; CRvB 13 July 1995, *RSV* 1996/3; CRvB 20 May 1997, *RSV* 1997/230.
108. See Jacobs A.T.J.M., *op. cit.*, p. 66; Schaub G., Arbeitsrechts-Handbuch, Munich, 1996, p. 2014; Gottwald P., Insolvenzrechts Handbuch, Munich, 1990, p. 1012.
109. Kania T., EK, §113 BetrVG Rn. 47; H. Wagner, Insolvenzrechtsreform: Neuerungen im Ablauf künftiger Insolvenzverfahren, *DStR*, 1996/5, p. 222.
110. See Kania T., *loc. cit.*, *DStR*, 1996/21, p. 835; Hanau and Kania, EK, §113 BetrVG Rn. 45/48.
111. Directive 75/129/EEC [1975] OJ L48/29.
112. Directive 92/56 EEC [1992] OJ L 245/3.
113. Directive 98/59/EC [1998] OJ L 225/16,

Britain, means that their legislation on the matter has largely been harmonized.[114] However, the original Directive of 1975 included an important restriction: in accordance with its Article 1(2)(d) it was not applicable in the event of company closure resulting from a judicial decision. In 1992 this was amended by Directive 92/56 in a manner which establishes beyond any doubt that it also applies in bankruptcy situations.[115] At the same time, in cases of bankruptcy the rules have been relaxed as regards two aspects:

- in accordance with the second sentence added to Article 3(1) in Directive 92/56, Member States may provide that, in the case of planned collective dismissals arising from the termination of business activities as a result of bankruptcy, the employer is obliged to notify the competent public authority in writing only if the latter so requests;
- in accordance with the paragraph 4 added to Article 4 in Directive 92/56, Member States need not apply the 30-day delay to collective dismissals arising from the termination of business activities as a result of bankruptcy.

In 1998 Directive 75/129/EEC and Directive 92/56/EEC were consolidated and replaced by Directive 98/59/EC.[116]

In the present study we therefore examine what use has been made by the four countries studied of the freedom given to them to moderate, in bankruptcy situations, the obligation to notify the competent authority and to observe the 30-day delay.

7.1 Obligation to notify the competent public authority

As regards the obligation to notify the competent public authority of any planned collective dismissals it may be observed that no use has been made by Belgium, Germany or Britain of the freedom offered in Article 3(1) of Directive 98/59 (former Directive 92/56) to make this optional in bankruptcy situations, with notification needing to take place only if the competent authority so requests. The procedure for notifying the competent public body – as well as the relevant trade unions – has not been modified.

In Belgium, for instance, a receiver who is planning to carry out collective dismissals must send notification of the fact to the head of the subregional Employment Office, supplying all the information normally stipulated.[117] Likewise in Britain, it makes no difference whether collective redundancies are being announced within the context of bankruptcy or outside it. The procedure for handling redundancies described in sections 188–198

114. Differences do still remain as a result of typical national specifics regarding a concept such as "collective redundancies" with respect to its scale (usually, dismissal of 20 employees or more), the precise identification of the employee representatives and public bodies to be informed and consulted and the manner in which things must be done.
115. Directive 92/56/EEC [1992] OJ L245/3.
116. [1998] OJ L 225/16.
117. See art. 7 Royal Decree of 24 May 1976 concerning collective dismissal.

TULR(C)A also applies in bankruptcy situations.[118] This means that collective redundancies arising from bankruptcy must still be notified to the Secretary of State for Employment in accordance with section 193 TULR(C)A, A similar observation can be made in the case of Germany: here, the legal rules applying to collective dismissals apply unchanged during bankruptcy. If the *Insolvenzverwalter* in Germany plans to carry out collective dismissals he must notify the fact to the local *Arbeitsamt*; he is obliged to make a formal declaration.[119]

Only in The Netherlands has use been made of the possibility of relaxing the obligation to notify the competent public authority.[120] Art. 3(1) Wmco (Wet Melding Collectief Ontslag) provides that in bankruptcy situations written notification of collective dismissals need be sent to the CWI only at the latter's own explicit request.[121] This seldom appears to happen in practice.

7.2 The 30-day delay

A potentially greater handicap for the receiver than the notification aspect discussed above is presented by the 30-day delay provided for in Article 4(1) of the Directive: the rule that the proposed dismissals cannot take effect until at least 30 days after the notification of the competent public authority. Not that the influence of this rule should be overestimated, however, because the Directive uses the concept of the time when collective redundancies may "take effect"; the time when "termination with notice" of the contracts may occur is not, as such, delayed. Given that notice periods of one month or longer will in any case apply for the majority of employees (see Section 5 above), normally the Article 4 rule will not necessarily create any insurmountable problems in practice. Added to this, in Directive 92/56 (now Directive 98/59/EC) the EC legislators subsequently gave Member States the freedom not to apply this rule in bankruptcy situations. How have the countries being studied here handled the matter?

In The Netherlands, for normal collective dismissals the Wmco is in principle more rigorous than the Directive, since – at least as a general rule – not even a *permit* to dismiss can be issued until a period of one month has elapsed after notification of the CWI. However, this rule has been waived for collective dismissals in bankruptcy situations, as no permit to dismiss is needed in bankruptcy cases (art. 2 Wmco juncto art. 6 BBA).

A comparable situation exists in Belgium. In cases involving company closure in the event of bankruptcy, the receiver need not observe the previously mentioned 30-day delay. He can terminate the contracts of employment immediately.[122]

118. Davies P., Insolvency and Employment Protection, *Industrial Law Journal* 1993/22, pp. 55–58.
119. §17 KSchG; Duwell J., *op. cit.*, p. 1047.
120. The notification of employee representatives is still obligatory even in bankruptcy situations.
121. Originally, there had been a formal obligation on the receiver to effect such notification.
122. See art. 9(2) Royal Decree of 24 May 1976 concerning collective dismissal.

In Germany, on the other hand, only subsidiary and not standard use has been made of the freedom offered by the Directive. The 30-day waiting period which for collective dismissals normally starts to run after due notification of the local *Arbeitsamt* (the so-called *Entlassungssperre*, see §18 KSchG) also applies in principle to collective dismissals in bankruptcy situations.[123] However, during this waiting period itself it is permissible for termination to take place, with the notice periods therefore already starting to run.[124] In addition, on the basis of §18 KSchG an exception to the general rule can be made if the A*rbeitsamt* grants authorization to effect dismissals earlier. These two factors combined mean that, in the case of Germany as well, the 30-day delay does not ultimately present a serious obstacle for the receiver.

The situation in Britain is somewhat similar. Here too the normal procedures prescribed for collective redundancies remain fully applicable in bankruptcy situations, although just as in Germany notice of termination of the contracts of employment can be issued during the consultation period itself, with the notice periods therefore already starting to run. One very real difference could, however, prove to lie in the fact that, in accordance with section 188(1) TULR(C)A, in Britain that consultation period lasts for not 30 days but actually 90 days in cases where the dismissal of 100 or more employees is proposed.

8. COMPARISON OF DISMISSALS LAW AND PROTECTION AGAINST DISMISSAL IN BANKRUPTCY SITUATIONS

Comparatively speaking, on the basis of the foregoing it may be said that in terms of dismissals law and protection against dismissal the fact of bankruptcy does not automatically terminate the relevant contracts of employment, without consequential effects, in any of the four countries studied. Although in Belgium and Britain the contracts can come to an end automatically, this has specified legal consequences. Apart from this, the receiver enjoys considerable freedom to carry out dismissals in all four of the countries studied.

Employees' protection against dismissal is extremely limited in the context of bankruptcy. Nowhere does the so-called *Entlassungssperre* against collective dismissals present any real obstacle, with the possible exception of situations in Britain involving the dismissal of 100 or more employees.

General bans on dismissal do not apply in bankruptcy situations, while specific bans on dismissal for specified categories of grounds for dismissal and dismissal situations play a role, at most, when the receiver is pursuing a strategy of selective dismissals. But whether in the event of selective dismissals a particular ban on dismissal has to be taken into account, and if so to what extent, is unclear in all four of the countries studied. The same is true of judicial control to ensure enforcement of the law: in principle this is of relevance, at most, in cases of selective dismissal, but precisely what that relevance amounts

123. Mönning R.-D., *op. cit.*, p. 210.
124. Jacobs A.T.J.M., *op.cit.*, p. 129 and Duwell J., *op. cit.*, p. 1057.

to is unclear. In Germany the practical implications were clear and the legislators have issued new rules to allow the receiver some room for manoeuvre. In the other three countries the existing formally prescribed scope for judicial testing would appear to have been little used in practice.

Otherwise, it is notable that the receiver who gets rid of all the employees at the same time – and is permitted to do so – has less to fear from the rules on dismissal than a receiver who decides on a strategy of selective dismissal!

As regards the costs associated with dismissal – periods of notice and compensation for dismissal or redundancy payments – there would appear to be fairly major differences between the four countries studied. It is striking, however, that in terms of both notice period and compensation for dismissal the receiver in The Netherlands comes off the most "cheaply". Since the introduction of the Wet Flexibiliteit en Zekerheid as from 1 January 1999 the periods of notice applied in The Netherlands are the shortest of those in all four countries. In addition, in The Netherlands the receiver is almost never obliged to pay compensation for dismissal and the guarantee institution likewise does not cover it. In the other countries studied either the receiver still has to bear the cost of compensation for dismissal to a greater or lesser extent as part of the liabilities or expenses of the estate or its payment is covered by the guarantee institutions.

5. Business Transfers in the Context of Bankruptcy

1. INTRODUCTION

It quite often happens that in the course of bankruptcy proceedings a receiver decides that (part of) the company operated by the bankrupt should be sold and transferred to a third party. In the present chapter we examine the question of the extent to which a transfer of this kind is affected by national or European rules regarding the rights and obligations of employees. In this connection in 1977 the EC Commission, following the model of existing legislative provisions in France and Germany regarding employees' rights in the event of transfers of undertakings, took an important step in this field. In Directive 77/187[1] it is stipulated that the rights and obligations which arise for the transferor from a contract of employment are *de jure* transferred to the transferee by reason of the transfer of a business. The main purpose of the Directive is to ensure that the restructuring of a company through its transfer to a third party does not have unduly adverse consequences for the employees involved. Dismissal purely *on the grounds of* the transfer itself is null and void; however, the provisions do not stand in the way of dismissal for economic, technical or organizational reasons.[2] The Directive therefore undeniably provides protection for the employees affected by a business transfer.[3]

Quite soon after its entry into force, however, uncertainty arose as to whether the Directive also applies in bankruptcy situations. This ultimately led to a judgment by the European Court of Justice in which it was held that the Directive itself did not apply to the transfers arising from a bankruptcy.[4] According to the Court, the rationale behind the decision was that if the Directive also applied in insolvency situations the European legislators would have included in it an express provision to that effect, given the considerable variation between the rules governing bankruptcy in the individual Member States. The Court did add, however, that Member States are at liberty to apply the principles of the Directive (in part) on their own initiative to all insolvency situations.

---

1. Directive 77/187/EEC [1997] OJ L61/126.
2. See art. 4(1) of the Directive; *cf.* ECJ Case 101/87 *Bork International* [1988] ECR 3057; also Pollard D., *Industrial Law Journal* 1996/25, pp. 191–211 at pp. 207–210.
3. EC Commission, COM(94) 300 final, 08.09.1994, p. 1.
4. ECJ Case 135/83 *Abels* [1985] ECR 469; *NJ* 1985, 900.

R. Blanpain, A.T.J.M. Jacobs (eds.), Employee Rights in Bankruptcy, 45–54.

In 1998 Directive 77/187 was amended by Directive 98/50.[5] Both Directives were consolidated by Council Directive 2001/23.[6] Since the 1998 Amendment Directive it is now specifically established that the core provisions of the Directive's Articles 3 and 4 do not apply in bankruptcy situations. However, the Member States are left free to provide otherwise, with a choice between various alternatives in the Directive. The Directive's other provisions, notably Articles 5 and 6 (information and consultation), are from now on also applicable during bankruptcy (see Chapter 6, Section 3 below). In addition, on the basis of Article 4a(4) of Directive 98/50 the Member States are required to take appropriate measures against any misuse of insolvency proceedings that could deprive employees of the rights accorded to them by the Directive.

The present chapter examines the extent to which, in the four legal systems studied (Germany, Belgium, Britain and The Netherlands), Directives 77/187 and 98/50 have been implemented and are applicable to bankruptcy situations.

2. BANKRUPTCY-RELATED BUSINESS TRANSFERS IN GERMANY

Germany already had a legislative provision in place, before the entry into force of Directive 77/187, stipulating that in the event of a business transfer the rights and obligations arising from contracts of employment are transferred to the transferee: §613a BGB. This article was adapted in 1980 to implement other aspects of the EU Directive.[7] In the late 1970s and early 1980s the question arose whether the §613a BGB rule was also applicable to transfers arising from bankruptcy. For instance, the *Bundesarbeitsgericht* (BAG) ruled that §613a BGB is also applicable in insolvency situations but added a limitation of liability in this context,[8] to the effect that the transferee is liable only for claims arising after the date of the bankruptcy judgment (so-called *Neuschulden*). The transferee is not liable for pre-existing claims dating from before the date of the bankruptcy. The purpose of this limitation of liability[9] was to avoid a situation where prospective purchasers are discouraged from buying a business in a bankruptcy context because they could be saddled with the burden of debts dating from before the bankruptcy.[10]

Despite this interpretation of the applicability of §613a BGB as being accompanied by a limitation of liability, not all of the associated problems were resolved. The fact that the transferee of a business in a bankruptcy context still

5. Directive 98/50/EC [1998] OJ L201/88.
6. Directive 2001/23/EC [2001] OJ L 82/16.
7. EG-Anpassungsgesetz of 13 August 1980, *BGBl.* I, p. 1308.
8. See BAG 17.1.1980, *AP* No. 18 concerning §613a BGB, *NJW* 1980, 1124. Also BAG 20.11.1984, *AP* No. 38 concerning §613a BGB, *DB* 1985, 1135 and BAG 4.12.1986, *AP* No. 56 concerning §613a BGB.
9. Schumacher R., Business Transfers and Insolvency, *Industrial Law Journal* 1994/23(1), pp. 101–107 at p. 103, and Kania T., *loc. cit.*, p. 835.
10. See *BGBL* I 1991 §54(858) and Stein L., Betriebsübergang im gesamtvollstreckungsverfahren, *EuZW* 1992/16, p. 506.

has to take over its entire workforce continued to be seen as an obstacle. Any subsequent reduction of the workforce was then possible only via Germany's (strict) dismissals law.[11] A situation still none too attractive for prospective purchasers, who may therefore continue to be put off by it – the result being, so the argument went, unnecessarily low bids for parts of businesses sold off in bankruptcy situations, something which is bad for the economy and for employment.[12] Consequently, in the new legislation on bankruptcy the legislators have, as from 1 October 1996/1 January 1999 in §125–128 InsO, gone another step farther as regards the applicability of §613a BGB.

In principle the validity of §613a BGB in insolvency situations has been maintained. However, in order to make a reduction of the workforce simpler and attract prospective purchasers of a business in a bankruptcy situation the new legislation introduces a relaxation of employment protection in the event of a bankruptcy-related transfer. To this end, §128(1) InsO states that the rules in §§125–127 InsO (on selective dismissals, see Chapter 4, Section 3 above) are also applicable to changes to the business that are not actually carried out until after it has been sold. Without this provision, the purchaser would have to wait until the receiver has carried out the changes before taking over the business because otherwise the opportunity for simplified dismissals is lost.[13] Furthermore, under §128(2) InsO the legal presumption is that dismissal at the time of a bankruptcy-related transfer is not by reason of the transfer. In such situations it is for the dismissed employee to prove otherwise.[14]

3. BANKRUPTCY-RELATED BUSINESS TRANSFERS IN BELGIUM

No legislation to protect employees in the event of a business transfer existed in Belgium prior to the entry into force of Directive 77/187. The Directive was implemented by means of a Collective Agreement concluded in 1985 within the Nationale Arbeidsraad (NAR) and subsequently decreed generally binding, which means that it is binding on the whole of Belgian business and industry.[15] This agreement safeguards the rights of the employees in the event of a change in the identity of the natural or legal person who operates the enterprise. As required by the Directive the Agreement provides that the transferee employer is obliged to observe the existing contracts of employment. Under its Article 7 employees' rights deriving from the contract of employment must be retained.

11. Jacobs A.T.J.M., Insolventierecht en sociaal recht – naar een nieuw evenwicht, *TvI* 1998/7, p. 160.
12. For example, Mönning R.-D., *op.cit.*, p. 217 even referred in this connection to a "Sword of Damocles" hanging over the head of a potential transferee.
13. Balz M., Die neue Insolvenzgesetze, Düssseldorf, 1995, p. 226.
14. Pick E., Die (neue) Insolvenzordnung – ein Überblick, *NJW*, 1995/15, p. 993 and Duwell J., *op. cit.*, p. 1122.
15. Nationale Arbeidsraad Collective Agreement No. 32bis, pronounced generally applicable by Royal Decree of 25 July 1985 (*BS*, 9-8-1985).

As regards the question of the applicability of the Agreement's provisions to bankruptcy-related transfers, Belgium has adopted a middle-of-the-road position.

On the one hand, it is assumed in Belgium that on the basis of the case-law of the European Court of Justice the provisions on automatic transfer in Title II of the Collective Agreement are not applicable to bankruptcy-related transfers, meaning that the transferee is free to decide whether employees are to be transferred to his employment, and if so which of the employees.[16] In contrast to the situation in a normal transfer, therefore, in bankruptcy situations the employees do not have a right to be transferred to the new employer.[17]

On the other hand, it is considered logical in Belgium that in so far as employees may keep their jobs as a consequence of the fact that the business in which they are employed is transferred by reason of bankruptcy, those employees should enjoy the same benefits after bankruptcy as employees in other transfer contexts, meaning that their rights and obligations arising from the contract of employment are retained unchanged with respect to the transferee.[18] Consequently, the transferee is under an obligation:

- to apply the collectively agreed or practised terms and conditions of employment applied by the bankrupt employer, failing any agreement with the unions to deviate from them;
- as regards individually agreed terms and conditions of employment, to include in all cases an employee's length of service under the former employer in the calculation of notice periods and compensation for dismissal.[19]

These special arrangements set out in Title III of Collective Agreement No. 32bis are applicable if the transfer of the business takes place within six months after the date of the bankruptcy and if the renewed employment commences within six months after the date of the transfer. The arrangements cover only those who on the date of the bankruptcy were employees or apprentices of the bankrupt (not agency workers) and also, subject to certain conditions, employees who had been dismissed not more than one month before the bankruptcy.[20]

Those employees who are transferred to the transferee under these arrangements can make an immediate claim for a bridging payment as provided for by the Law of 12 April 1985[21] for the time which their employment has been interrupted. This payment is intended to replace the income lost over that period and is paid out by the Sluitingsfond.[22] The

16. See arts. 6 and 12 Nationale Arbeidsraad Collective Agreement No. 32bis.
17. Blanpain R. and Vanachter O., *op. cit.*, p. 198.
18. Sociaal Commentaarboekje 1996–97, Diegem, 1997, p. 263.
19. See arts. 11–15 Title III Nationale Arbeidsraad Collective Agreement No. 32bis.
20. See art. 11 Nationale Arbeidsraad Collective Agreement No. 32bis; *cf.* Rasschaert K. et al., *op. cit.*, pp. 263–263.
21. *BS*, 19-6-1985.
22. Arts. 1 and 9 Law of 12 April 1985, *BS*, 19-6-1985. If the Sluitingsfonds pays out a bridging payment, in contrast to other recovery claims (see Chapter 2 above) the resultant claim against the bankrupt estate is not preferential.

procedure for claiming a bridging payment is regulated in Article 11 of the 1985 Law and the associated Royal Decree of 17 July 1985.[23] To be eligible, an employee must satisfy two conditions:

- on the date of the bankruptcy he must have been covered by a contract of employment or apprenticeship contract, or have been dismissed during the preceding month with entitlement to compensation for dismissal which on that date was not being paid or paid only in part;
- he must be transferred at the time when the assets are transferred or within a period of six months thereafter.[24]

The amount of the bridging payment is equal to the gross pay formerly received by the employee, subject to a monthly maximum of 1,825 Euro.[25] The period with respect to which it is payable is the interval between the interruption of the company's business activity and the commencement of employment with the new employer.[26] Entitlement to the payment is forfeited if the employee fails to make use of the opportunity of employment with the transferee,[27] and also if during the transitional period the employee performs paid work for the receiver or for a third party. In addition, it is not paid if the Sluitingsfonds is already paying out compensation for dismissal.[28] The receipt of a bridging payment precludes compensation payable by reason of company closure.[29]

4. BANKRUPTCY-RELATED BUSINESS TRANSFERS IN BRITAIN

Likewise in Britain, at the time of the entry into force of Directive 77/187 there were no statutory provisions on the issue of employees' rights in the event of business transfers. The Directive was subsequently implemented through the introduction of the Transfer of Undertakings (Protection of Employment) Regulations 1981 (TUPE).[30] In conformity with the Directive, it is stipulated under TUPE that in the event of a business transfer the rights and obligations arising from a contract of employment are transferred from the transferor to the transferee.[31] Dismissal by reason of a business transfer is not permitted; in accordance with section 8 TUPE it is treated as unfair dismissal.

As regards the issue of a bankruptcy-related business transfer, the view taken in Britain, just as in Belgium, is that the purchaser of a business is free to choose whether he wishes to take employees into his employment, and if so

23. *BS*, 21-8-1985.
24. Art. 5 Law of 12 April 1985, *BS*, 19-6-1985.
25. Art. 8 Law of 12 April 1985, *BS*, 19-6-1985.
26. Art. 4 Law of 12 April 1985, *BS*, 19-6-1985.
27. Rasschaert K. et al., *op. cit.*, p. 263.
28. Art. 7 Law of 12 April 1985, *BS*, 19-6-1985.
29. See Chapter 4, Section 6 above. The employee can however claim compensation for dismissal chargeable to his former employer despite receiving a bridging payment. To do so, the employee must file his claim in the bankruptcy proceedings of his former employer. See Arbeidshof Brussels 6 April 1990, *Soc. Kron.*, 1991, 28.
30. Amended in 1992 (TULR(C)A) and 1995 (SI 1995/2587).
31. See section 5 TUPE; *cf.* Jefferson M., *op. cit.*, p. 328.

which employees.[32] In this sense, therefore, there is no automatic transfer of the workforce in the event of a business transfer. But in so far as the workforce is taken into employment with the transferee employer, the latter is required to observe the rights and obligations of the "transferred" employees.

5. BANKRUPTCY-RELATED BUSINESS TRANSFERS IN THE NETHERLANDS

Likewise in The Netherlands, at the time of the entry into force of Directive 77/187 there were no statutory provisions in force on the issue of employees' rights in the event of a business transfer. The Directive was subsequently introduced into national legislation through the insertion of Articles 1639aa *et seq.* BW, now Articles 7:662–666 BW.[33] In conformity with the Directive, it is laid down in art. 7:663 BW that in the event of transfer of an enterprise the rights and obligations arising from the employment relationship between the employees who work in the enterprise and the employer (who is transferring the enterprise) are *de jure* transferred to the new owner.

The applicability or otherwise of these provisions to transfers effected in the context of bankruptcy proceedings became the subject of heated debate in The Netherlands in the 1980s.[34] Not only as regards whether the BW provisions apply but also whether, if the answer is yes, they would free the guarantee institutions from the obligation to take on the payment liabilities of a former employer in cases of his inability to pay.[35] It was argued that if the BW provisions applied in bankruptcy situations it would mean that prospective purchasers of (parts of) bankrupt businesses would be dissuaded from proceeding if the existing contracts of employment are automatically transferred to the enterprise they are acquiring, saddling them with the debts of the business to be transferred with all of the employees concerned. This would reduce the chances of successful transfers, with the concomitant – unfavourable – repercussions on employment.[36] The uncertainty subsequently led to disputes, in the context of which various courts[37] submitted references for a preliminary ruling on the matter to the European Court of Justice. In reply the Court ruled in 1985 that Directive 77/187 does not apply to a bankruptcy-related transfer.[38] This still did not in itself definitely establish whether this interpretation was also valid in The Netherlands, but shortly

32. Jefferson M., *op. cit.*, p. 333.
33. Law of 15 May 1981, *Stb.* 1981, 400.
34. For an overview, see Lodder H., De artikelen 1639aa e.v. BW en het faillissement, *Ars Aequi* 1988/4, p. 223.
35. See on this point Chapter 3 above; *cf.* CRvB 29 April 1986, WW 1983/714, *RSV* 1986/171.
36. van het Kaar R.H. and Knegt R., Doorstart na faillissement: de positie van werknemers, *NJB* 1996/39, p. 1624; Christe D., Arbeidsovereenkomst Kluwer, Afdeling 8, Rechten van de werknemer bij overgang van een onderneming, Suppl. 175, April 1997, art. 7:666–1 and Joosen E.P.M., Overdracht van ondernemingen uit faillissement, Deventer, 1998, p. 204.
37. For example, Rechtbank Den Haag (16 August 1983, *NJ* 1984, 356) and Kantonrecht Rotterdam (25 August 1983, *NJ* 1984, 357).
38. In three cases decided on the same day: ECJ 7 February 1985, *NJ* 1985, 900–902.

afterwards the Hoge Raad also ruled that the BW articles on business transfers were not applicable in bankruptcy situations.[39] In the course of the recodification of labour law in Book 7 BW this decision has been incorporated by the legislators into the present art. 7:666 BW. Against this background there arose in The Netherlands a legal situation, which differs from that in the other three countries studied. Not only is the transferee acquiring an enterprise in a bankruptcy context free, under Netherlands law, to choose whether to have employees transferred to his employment, and if so which employees, but he is also under no obligation to continue to offer those employees who are transferred to his employment the same rights and obligations as those which they had with respect to their former employer. In short, in a bankruptcy-related transfer the transferee has complete freedom.

Criticisms of the situation as it exists in The Netherlands have certainly been voiced during recent years.[40] Arguments advocating, with varying degrees of caution, partial application of the legal regime laid down in arts. 7:662 ff. BW to bankruptcy-related transfers have in the meantime been advanced by a number of authors.[41] In practice, however, there has been little evidence of any shift in approach. The only signs are that in the case of an employee who is initially taken into employment by the purchaser of a business in bankruptcy but then nevertheless dismissed several first-instance courts have shown a tendency to count his length of service with the bankrupt employer towards the calculation of his subsequent compensation for dismissal.[42] Furthermore, it is conceivable that arts. 7:662 ff. BW could still apply in situations of purely "technical" or "orchestrated" bankruptcy.[43] There is certainly a growing body of opinion calling for more measures against "fraudulent insolvency

39. HR 30 October 1987, *NJ* 1988, 191.

40. See, for example, van het Kaar R.H. and Knegt R., *loc. cit.*, p. 1627; van Eeghen L.J., Verkenning van belangen bij doorstart na faillissement, *TVVS* 1996/4, pp. 93–98; Lennarts M.L. and van Straalen P.W., Toepassing van de artt. 7A: 1639aa e.v. BW, ook in faillissement?, *TVVS* 1997/1. pp. 1–6; Vriesendorp R.D., Doorstarten en onbehoorlijk bestuur, in: Vriesendorp R.D. (ed.), Onbehoorlijk bestuur in het insolventierecht, Insolad Jaarboek 1997, Deventer, 1997, pp. 65–82. *Cf.* de Ranitz S.H., Beroepsethiek in insolventieland, *Advocatenblaad* 1995/5, pp. 198–200 and the *TVVS* special issue "Doorstart", *TVVS* 1997/7, plus van Straalen P.W., Behoud van rechten van werknemers bij overgang van onderneming, Deventer, 1996, chapter 6 and in particular §6.6 and 6.7.

41. Grapperhaus F.B.J., *ArbeidsRecht* 1996/71, p. 12; Luttmer-Kat A.M., *TvI* 1997/2, p. 47; Joosen E.P.M., *op. cit.*, pp. 205–207 as well as some authors mentioned in the previous footnote.

42. Kantongerecht Leiden 22 March 1995, reg. No. 89/95, Kantongerecht Utrecht 3 May 1995, reg. No. 43598 and Kantongerecht Groningen 29 September 1995, *JAR* 1996/103. *Cf.* Lasschuit D., De Wet Overgang Ondernemingen en faillissement, *Advocatenblad* 1996/4, p. 151 and Knüppe B.F.M., De doorstart en de Richtlijnen 77/187/EEC and 98/50/EC, in: A.M. Luttmer-Kat (ed.), *op. cit.*, p. 58.

43. *Cf.* Rechtbank Utrecht 9 December 1992, *JAR* 1993/57; Hof Den Haag 10 January 1996, *JOR* 1996/16 (Ammerlaan); Vriesendorp R.D., in: Vriesendorp R.D. (ed.), *op. cit.*, pp. 67 *ff.*; Loesberg E., in: Luttmer-Kat A.M. (ed.), *op. cit.*, p. 20. Apart from the difficulties here of producing the necessary proof, the problem often remains that the legal person is nevertheless in a state of cessation of payments and that a bankruptcy is therefore unavoidable (arts. 1 and 6(3) Fw.); *cf.* the note by Kortmann S.C.J.J. in *JOR* 1996/16. See also Oosthout H.B., *op. cit.*, §7.4.3.

proceedings", as is also required under the new Directive 2001/23/EC (former Directive 98/50).[44]

6. COMPARISON OF THE VARIOUS SYSTEMS AS REGARDS BANKRUPTCY-RELATED BUSINESS TRANSFERS

In all four of the countries studied the basic idea underlying Directive 2001/23/EC (former Directives 77/187/EEC and 98/50/EC) – the retention of employees' rights in the event of transfers of undertakings – has run up against the harsh reality of bankruptcy. To include bankruptcy situations in an uncompromising enforcement of that idea would discourage prospective purchasers of a business in a bankruptcy context, something that serves the interests of neither the employees nor the creditors. The same is consequently true as regards employment and the economy in general. It is therefore not surprising that the applicability of the rules on business transfers to a bankruptcy context has been the subject of provisos. What is more, the judgments delivered by the European Court of Justice in 1985 offered the scope to do so. The system in which this scope has been taken to its extreme is in Netherlands law: first by the courts and later by the legislators. They establish quite categorically that the rules on the protection of employees' rights do not apply to transfers arising from bankruptcy. In comparison with the other countries studied here this could be described as "overkill", since the latter have all opted for less extreme, middle-of-the-road solutions.

In Belgium and Britain, although the non-applicability of the Directive's rules to bankruptcy situations has been taken as a starting-point there is also provision to the effect that these rules must be applied in part to the legal position of employees who are taken into employment by a purchaser of a part of a business as a result of a bankruptcy. And in the case of Belgium it is also notable that the system provides an attractive "bridging payment" for employees who are subsequently taken into employment by the purchaser of a business in a bankruptcy situation. In Germany, the opposite route has been taken in eventually arriving at what likewise amounts to a midway position. The view taken is that, in principle, the rules on business transfers are also applicable to bankruptcy-related transfers. However, this applicability is not unconditional, because first the courts imposed a limitation on liability in such contexts and then, more recently, the legislators introduced a relaxation of the protection against dismissal provided for those employees who are transferred to the new employer.

The Netherlands implementation of the Directive compares poorly with these other national provisions.

44. See art. 5(4) Directive 2001/23/EC. On this question see, among others: Vriesendorp R.D. (ed.), *op.cit.*, pp. 78–81; van Straalen P.W., *op. cit.*, p. 106; Bloemarts J.C.M.G., in: Luttmer-Kat A.M. (ed.), *op. cit.*, p. 74; van der Voet G.W., Misbruik van faillissementsrecht bij overgang van onderneming, Rotterdam, 2000. A cautious view is taken by Knüppe B.F.M., in: Luttmer-Kat A.M. (ed.), *op. cit.*, p. 57; see also van der Voet G.W., Misbruik van faillissementsrecht bij overgang van onderneming, Rotterdam, 2000.

7. NEW DEVELOPMENTS

A number of legal systems provide for reorganization procedures which function as a kind of "pre-bankruptcy" state, such as the *surséance van betaling* procedure in The Netherlands [judicial leave to suspend payment of debts with a view to reaching a settlement]. This raises the question whether the exclusion of bankruptcy situations from the Directive's rules on transfers also operates in the case of such pre-bankruptcy reorganization procedures. If the answer is no, it sharpens the distinction between bankruptcy and a reorganization procedure.

In the 1990s the European Court of Justice ruled that Directive 77/187 does also apply to transfers in the context of reorganization procedures.[45] Nevertheless, some degree of scope for Member States also to exempt such procedures from the general rules on transfers has been incorporated into the amended Directive 98/50 (now: Directive 2001/23/EC). This new development is prompting the national legislators to consider whether they wish to make use of this new opportunity and, in the same connection, to give fresh thought to whether they wish to maintain their existing law on the subject of the applicability of the transfer rules at the bankruptcy stage. In the meantime debate on the matter has got under way in The Netherlands, as elsewhere.[46]

45. See Case C-362/89 *d'Urso* [1991] ECR I-4105 and Case C-472/93 *Spano* [1995] ECR I-4321; *cf.* Beltzer R., Insolvente ondernemingen en werknemers in transitie, in: v. d. Heijden P.F. et. al., Naar een nieuwe rechtsorde van de arbeid, Deventer, 1999, pp. 92–94.

46. See, recently, Beltzer R., *loc. cit.*, p. 81 and van Straalen P.W., *op. cit.*, Chapter 6.

6. Participation Rights in Bankruptcy

1. INTRODUCTION

In this chapter we examine the manner in which employee participation is able to take place in a company where the (legal) person concerned is in a state of bankruptcy. Participation can materialize in two forms: via the trade unions and/or via elected representative bodies (works council/*Betriebsrat*). What are the rights and powers of unions and works councils in a bankruptcy situation? What are the legislative provisions on the matter in The Netherlands, Belgium, Germany and Britain?[1] To this end, in the following sections a study is made of how participation is regulated for unions and works councils with respect to the bankruptcy petition itself (Section 2) and with respect to the decisions which are made by the receiver in the course of the bankruptcy proceedings and in which employees' rights and interests are at stake (Section 3). In this latter case it is primarily a question of decisions on dismissal or continued employment and the sale of (part of) the company.

The investigation is confined to the legal situation in larger companies, since in Germany and The Netherlands works councils have the most rights in enterprises employing, respectively, more than 100 and more than 50 employees, while in Belgium it is only where there are 100 or so more employees that works councils function in practice to their full extent.

2. PARTICIPATION AND THE BANKRUPTCY PETITION

A distinction has to be drawn here between the situation where the bankruptcy petition is submitted by the debtor himself and that where it is submitted by third parties (creditors). In the latter case third parties are hardly likely to inform or consult unions and works councils in advance. By contrast, participation does come into the picture where the bankruptcy petition is submitted by the (legal) person/debtor himself. What is said below relates to this situation.

In Belgium the company management must, on pain of a fine, give notification of the bankruptcy petition, together with the reasons for it, to the works council or, where there is no works council, to the workplace health and safety committee, the "union delegation" or a "workforce representative

1. In the case of Britain it should be noted that participation via the works council is out of the question, since Britain has no statutory system of works councils. Consequently, participation is possible there only via the unions, whereas in the three other countries participation can materialize both via the unions and via the works councils.

R. Blanpain, A.T.J.M. Jacobs (eds.), Employee Rights in Bankruptcy, 55–62.

body", at the very latest at the time when the petition is filed with the court.[2] The purpose of this obligation is to allow discussion within the works council of the petition and the reasons for it. It cannot, however, block or delay the petition in any way. Given that the discussions with the works council have no further influence on the bankruptcy petition, the obligation does not amount to prior consultation.[3] There is, nevertheless, some cause for doubt. Petitioning for bankruptcy is, unquestionably, an internal decision with significant repercussions for the company. Hence, this decision falls within the scope of art. 25 of the Royal Decree of 27 November 1973 on the provision of information to works councils, which means that the bankruptcy petition must be communicated and explained to the council as far *in advance* as possible.[4] Furthermore, Belgian law recognizes a general obligation on the management to inform and consult with the works council "in good time and before any public announcement".[5] The question has now arisen as to how these pre-existing provisions relate to the new art. 9 of the 1997 Faillissementswet. It is, as yet, an open question whether an employer who complies strictly with the Faillissementswet, not informing the works council until the time at which the bankruptcy petition is filed in court, is in breach of his obligations under the Royal Decree of 27 November 1973 and the Nationale Arbeidsraad Collective Agreement No. 9; or does art. 9 of the Faillissementswet take precedence as *lex specialis*?[6]

In The Netherlands there are no specific provisions obliging the employer to inform the works council of a bankruptcy petition. The council certainly might make use of art. 10 Fw. in order to lodge an objection within a period of eight days after the bankruptcy judgment.[7] It is also arguable that the general right to information enjoyed by the works council on the basis of art. 31 WOR also applies to a bankruptcy petition, signifying an obligation on the employer to inform the works council of a bankruptcy judgment immediately. For a long time there was uncertainty as regards how far a decision on the part of the employer to submit a bankruptcy petition himself is subject to the works council's consultation right (*adviesrecht*) ex art. 25 WOR.[8] In 1980 the Rechtbank Den Bosch delivered a judgment answering this question in the

2. See art. 9 of the new Faillissementswet of 8 August 1997 (*BS*, 28–10–1997).
3. Rasschaert K. and Veys F., *loc. cit.*, p. 198; Rasschaert K. et al., *op. cit.*, p. 341.
4. The works council is firstly entitled to business and financial information, including not just regular information but so-called "occasional information" on events or internal decisions that could have significant repercussions for the company. It also has information rights on labour-related issues, such as those which could undoubtedly be associated with a bankruptcy petition.
5. See art. 11 Nationale Arbeidsraad Collective Agreement No. 9 concerning works councils, dating from 9 March 1972.
6. Rasschaert K. et al., *op. cit.*, p. 242.
7. As stated by Loesberg E., in: A.M. Luttmer Kat (ed.), *op. cit.*, p. 21. Bloemarts J.C.M.G., in: A.M. Luttmer Kat (ed.), *op. cit.*, p. 74 doubts whether this is possible without further measures by the legislators, now that the works council has no capacity to initiate legal proceedings beyond the scope of WOR.
8. With respect to a number of economic and organizational decisions the employer is under an obligation to request an opinion from the works council in advance. This opinion must be requested in time enough for it to have a "real influence" on the proposed decision (art.

negative.[9] In 2000 the Dutch Supreme Court delivered a ruling denying the works council a right on information and consultation on requests for judicial leave to suspend payments in insolvency procedures.[10] The motivation for this judgment makes it unlikely that the Supreme Court will issue a different judgment with respect to bankruptcy petitions. Moreover, it may be asked whether a right to be consulted in advance can prove to be of any importance at all in practice, given the considerable time pressure involved where the employer himself submits a bankruptcy petition.[11]

In Germany information and consultation regarding a bankruptcy petition submitted by the employer himself fall within the scope of the general right to information and consultation conferred on the *Betriebsrat* under the Betriebsverfassungsgesetz.

3. PARTICIPATION AND DECISIONS BY THE RECEIVER

As regards decisions made by the receiver in the course of bankruptcy proceedings, before discussing the different countries separately it is useful to indicate the relevant European legislation. First, the EC Directive on collective redundancies[12] contains provisions on the information and consultation of employee representatives, which also apply in the event of collective dismissals in bankruptcy situations. In addition, the amended EC Directive on transfers of undertakings[13] merely offers the possibility of excluding its Articles 3 and 4 in bankruptcy situations, which means that its other provisions, including those concerning the information and consultation of employee representatives, do definitely apply to bankruptcy-related business transfers.

In Britain there is little or no traditional provision giving rise to a statutory right to the information and consultation of employee representatives. The only provisions that exist relate to collective redundancies and business transfers and have been introduced as a result of the obligation to do so imposed by the EC Directives on the subject. For example, the procedure

25(2) WOR). Examples of such decisions include cessation of the operation of the company or a part thereof (art. 25(c) WOR) or the retrenchment, expansion or other significant alteration of its activities (art. 25(d) WOR).

9. Rechtbank Den Bosch 9 April 1980, *NJ* 1980, 546. On this point see, for example, Kroft W.P.J., De curator en de medezeggenschap van werknemers, in: S.C.J.J. Kortmann *et al.*, De curator, een octopus, Deventer, 1996, p. 52. *Cf.* Broekman M.F.H., De ondernemingsraad en faillissement, *ArbeidsRecht* 1999/4, p. 8. The issue was expressly not examined by the OK (Amsterdam Court of Appeal/Companies Bench) in its judgment of 21 November 1996, *NJ* 1998, 502.

10. Hoge Raad 6 juni 2001, JAR 2001/128.

11. Although according to Roelvink H.L.J., from what he says in his argument against Kroft W.P.J., in: *TvI* 1997/1, p. 19 (see also p. 20), there is no cause for pessimism.

12. See art. 2 Directive 75/129/EEC [1975] OJ L 48/29 dating from 22 February 1975, amended by Directive 92/56/EEC of 24 June 1992 [1992] OJ L245/3; now consolidated and replaced by Directive 98/59/EC of 20 July 1998 [1998] OJ L 225/16; see, on this question, Chapter 4, Section 7 above.

13. Directive 98/50/EC of 29 June 1998 [1998] OJ L201/88, which amended Directive 77/187/EEC [1997] OJ L61/26; now consolidated and replaced by Directive 2001/23/EC of 12 March 2001 [2001] L 82/16. See, on this subject, Chapter 5 above.

laid down in sections 188–198 TULR(C)A applies where an employer is proposing to dismiss, on the grounds of redundancy, 20 or more employees within a period of 90 days or less.[14] This procedure takes place during a consultation period in which consultations must be held with the unions with a view, for example, to avoiding the dismissals, reducing the number of employees to be dismissed or mitigating the consequences of the dismissals eventually carried out.[15] For the purposes of effective consultation, the employer must disclose to the unions the information they need in order to be able to perform their function properly, such as the proposed method of selecting the employees to be dismissed and the reasons for the proposed dismissals.[16] This procedure is also incumbent upon the receiver/administrator/liquidator in bankruptcy situations.

In the case of The Netherlands the starting assumption is that the normal rules on employee participation must be observed by the receiver in a bankruptcy situation, given that within the meaning of the Works Council Act (WOR) the receiver is classed as the employer.[17] This means that decisions by the receiver regarding dismissals, closure of the enterprise, sale of company assets, etc. must be submitted to the works council for its opinion in accordance with art. 25 WOR.[18] If the works council's opinion is an unfavourable one, on the basis of art. 26 WOR the receiver would be unable to implement the decision concerned if the council lodges an appeal against it before the Amsterdam Court of Appeal/Enterprises Bench. However, no known case-law exists on instances of a receiver ever having been found guilty by the Court of Appeal/Enterprises Bench of failing to comply with the rules on participation. This might suggest that in practice receivers follow the rules. What seems more likely is that the participation bodies accept that the WOR obligations will not be fulfilled in the special circumstances of bankruptcy or that they feel there is little chance of a successful appeal to the Amsterdam Court of Appeal/Enterprises Bench on the grounds of the receiver's failure to request their opinion.[19]

Alongside the WOR, the Wet melding collectief ontslag (Wmco) also plays a part in The Netherlands as regards participation.[20] Under arts. 3 and 4

---

14. See Harvey, *op. cit.*, nos. 1–11.
15. See section 188(2) TULR(C)A.
16. See section 188(4) TULR(C)A.
17. See art. 1(1)(d)WOR. *Cf.* Kortmann S.C.J.J., De positie van de vennootschapsorganen, de ondernemingsraad en de curator tijdens faillissement, in: Van vennootschapsrechtelijk belang, Deventer, 1988, pp. 111–112 and De curator, de bewindwoerder en de organen van de vennootschap en onderneming, in: Het faillissement in de tijd van Molengraaff en nu. Proposals issued by Vereeniging "Handelsrecht", 1993, p. 156; Roest J., Medezeggenschap van werknemers bij financieel-economische besluiten, Amsterdam, 1996, p. 262; Kroft W.P.J., *loc. cit.*, pp. 55–58; Broekman M.F.H., *loc. cit.*, p. 10; Bloemarts J.C.M.G., in: A.M. Luttmer-Kat (ed.), *op. cit.*, pp. 76–77.
18. *Cf.* Companies Division (OK) Hof Amsterdam 21 November 1996, *NJ* 1998, 502, in which the OK left the matter undecided on a general basis, although an obligation to seek the council's opinion seems to be assumed.
19. *Cf.* Kroft W.P.J., *loc.cit.*, pp. 53–54; Knüppe B.F.M. at the Insolad Quinquennial Congress in 1996, reported in *TvI* 1997/1, p, 20; Dorresteijn A.F.M., *loc. cit.*, TvI 1999/3, p. 56 and *TvI* 2000/1, p. 35.
20. *Stb.* 1976, 233; amended *Stb.* 1993, 386.

Wmco notification must be sent to the trade unions for consultation purposes before collective dismissals can be carried out.[21] In bankruptcy situations this must be done by the receiver. When such consultation with the unions has been carried out in good time with favourable results and the other requirements laid down by the Wmco have been met, collective dismissals by the receiver can take place immediately.

Information and consultation of the unions in the event of the transfer of a large company is provided for in the Fusiegedragsregels [Code of Practice on Mergers] issued by the Social and Economic Council (SER) in 1975[22] and recently revised.[23] Since the Code of Practice is also applicable to a business transfer involving a bankruptcy-related assets transaction, consultation with the unions is also necessary in such situations.[24]

In Belgium it is likewise the case that the receiver usually makes a number of decisions, which, if being made by an employer,[25] are unquestionably subject to the works council's information and consultation rights.[26] These are decisions on the closure, transfer of ownership and retrenchment of the company entailing collective dismissals, forms of reorganization, changes in arrangements on working hours, etc. In addition, a receiver who decides to continue operating "business activities" must engage in consultations with the representative unions or, in their absence, with the existing workforce.[27] There also seems no doubt that the Royal Decree of 24 May 1976 and Nationale Arbeidsraad Collective Agreement No. 24[28] must be complied with before collective dismissals may take place in bankruptcy situations as well. This means that the receiver, too, must provide information and engage in consultations beforehand.[29] Only when he has fulfilled all these obligations can he proceed with collective dismissals.[30]

In Germany the role of the *Betriebsrat* is a major one. For instance, under §17 KSchG in cases of collective dismissal the employer is obliged to provide the *Betriebsrat* with information, in writing, on aspects such as the

21. *Cf.* Bijl. Hand T.K. 1992–93, 22970, No. 3, p. 2; see also Loesberg E., *loc. cit.*, *TvI*, 1998/4, p. 74 and Oosthout H.B., *op. cit.*, p. 84.
22. *Mededelingenblad SER* 9 December 1975, No. 43 (later amended).
23. See SER-Decision Code of Practice on Mergers 2000 to protect the interests of employees, 17 March 2000.
24. de Liagre Böhl E.W.J.H., Sanering en Faillissement, Deventer, 1991.
25. For the definition of the concept of employer (*ondernemer*) in this context, see art. 14 under 1 Wet op de Ondernemingsraden (section IV of the Law of 20 September 1948 on the Organization of the Economy, *BS* 27/28–9–1948).
26. Under art. 15(a) Wet op de Ondernemingsraden and art. 10 Nationale Arbeidsraad Collective Agreement No. 9 the works council issues opinions on all measures that are likely to change the organization of the work, working conditions and output, in which it may make suggestions and raise objections.
27. See Rasschaert K. et al., *op. cit.*, p. 242.
28. Pronounced generally binding via Royal Decree of 21 January 1976 (*BS*, 17–2–1976).
29. See art. 6 Nationale Arbeidsraad Collective Agreement No. 24. This control is important because the Renault affair demonstrated that employers do not always observe the stipulated provisions regarding collective dismissals; see, on this, Kolvenbach W., Massenentlassungen bei Renault in Belgien, *NZA*, 1997/13, pp. 695–697.
30. Sociaal Commentaarboekje, *op. cit.*, p. 249 and Blanpain R. and Vanachter O., *op. cit.*, p. 242; Balthazar T., Collectief ontslag, Aanwerven Tewerkstellen Ontslaan, Issue No. 29 (April 1993), pp. 301–1472.

reasons for dismissals and the number of employees to be involved. In addition consultations must be held with the *Betriebsrat* concerning the possibilities of avoiding dismissals or reducing their number and mitigating their consequences as far as possible. The information provided to the *Betriebsrat,* and the latter's views on the matter, must also be communicated by the employer to the local *Arbeitsamt*. In addition to these powers conferred by §17 KSchG, the *Betriebsrat* also retains those it possesses by virtue of §102 BetrVG regarding a proposed dismissal.[31] Furthermore, the *Betriebsrat* possesses information and consultation rights in economic matters. These apply to so-called *Betriebsänderungen*, i.e. cutbacks, closures, collective dismissals and mergers.[32] A "transfer of an undertaking" usually falls under this heading.[33] The *Betriebsrat*'s participation relates not so much to the business decision *per se* as to its labour-related consequences.[34] Its involvement is directed primarily at reaching agreement on a so-called *Interessenausgleich*.[35] This also entails the drawing-up of a "social plan".[36] If no agreement can be reached in this respect, an attempt must be made at arbitration, with the Director of the *Landesarbeitsamt* possibly being called on to mediate.

In bankruptcy situations the question arises how far, if at all, the position of the *Betriebsrat* alters. Certainly, in these circumstances the receiver often finds himself forced to take essential measures which fall under the heading of *Betriebsänderungen*, such as closing down or disposing of the business. Under the former legislation in force up till 1 October 1996/1 January 1999 all of the *Betriebsrat*'s participation rights were fully applicable to

31. See Chapter 4, Section 2 above.
32. See §111 BetrVG.
33. See Neef K., Betriebsübergang und Sozialplanregelung, *NZA* 1998/15, p. 804 and Neef K., Betriebsübergang und Betriebsänderung, *NZA* 1994/3, p. 97.
34. Jacobs A.T.J.M., *op. cit.*, p. 173.
35. The *Interessenausgleich* relates to the economic decision on a proposed major change to the business, as regards whether it should be implemented at all and if so in what way. For example, in the case of the introduction of new technologies the approach chosen via the *Interessenausgleich* may be to spread their introduction over a longer period so that more of the staff reductions involved can take place through natural wastage. Although reaching agreement on an *Interessenausgleich* is purely voluntary the provisions do not leave the employer entirely free: if he makes no attempt to reach such an agreement those employees dismissed as a result of the change to the business are entitled to compensation (§113(3) BetrVG); and once any such agreement is reached if he fails to abide by it without compelling reason the individual employees can in this case also claim compensation (§113(1) BetrVG). *Cf.* Lousberg E.J.H.M., Bescherming van arbeid in het licht van nieuwe technologieën, Lelystad, 1997, p. 137 and Koning G., Nieuwe technologieën en werknemersinspraak, Lelystad, 1998, p. 78.
36. The social consequences of *Betriebsänderungen* are usually regulated in a "social plan", which normally follows the *Interessenausgleich*. In Germany the *Betriebsrat* has a right to such a plan, which is defined in §112 BetrVG as an agreement drawn up to compensate or reduce the disadvantages suffered by employees as a result of the proposed change to the business. It has mandatory force: both employees and the *Betriebsrat* can apply to the courts for the enforcement of its provisions. As in The Netherlands, a German "social plan" often contains rules on compensation for dismissal. In accordance with case-law, in the event of job losses it performs a compensatory, bridging and welfare function for the period following the dismissal; see, for example, BAG *DB* 1979, 262; BAGE(GS) 31.176 (188), *AP* No. 6 re §112 BetrVG 1972.

bankruptcy-related *Betriebsänderungen* on the part of the receiver.[37] This was considered by many to be an obstacle standing in the way of the rescue or transfer of the bankrupt company.[38] As a result, under the present-day *Insolvenzordnung* such measures have been simplified when they take place in a bankruptcy context.

Although in principle the system of the *Interessenausgleich* and the "social plan" still remains also applicable to changes to the business carried out by the receiver, the legislation now makes it clear that the receiver and the *Betriebsrat* must enter into negotiations over any so-called *Betriebsvereinbarungen* (agreements reached between employer and works council) if the latter provide for benefits that may be chargeable to the estate.[39] However, if after three weeks' negotiations an *Interessenausgleich* has still not been reached, in order to speed up matters §121 InsO allows the attempt at arbitration to be omitted and on the basis of §122 InsO the receiver can make an immediate application to the *Arbeitsgericht* for permission, nevertheless, to carry out the *Betriebsänderungen* in question. By virtue of §112(2) BetrVG the *Arbeitsgericht* grants such permission if the company's financial position, even taking the employees' social interests into account, is such as to warrant the changes to the business being implemented without any possibility of appeal by the employees. In accordance with §113(3) BetrVG the grant of such permission by the *Arbeitsgericht* also precludes any right to compensation. If, on the other hand, the consultation procedure between receiver and *Betriebsrat* does result in agreement on an *Interessenausgleich* containing a list of the employees who are being dismissed for operational reasons, §125 InsO stipulates that the dismissal of those employees is legally valid.[40] The preliminary testing of dismissals by the *Betriebsrat* would thus appear to be precluded.[41]

4. COMPARISON OF PARTICIPATION RIGHTS IN BANKRUPTCY SITUATIONS

Employee participation and bankruptcy seem to be two things, which are difficult to reconcile with each other. An area of tension between them can be observed in all four of the countries studied. Britain differs in that the tension is not all that apparent, but this is also because in the bankruptcy context participation plays scarcely any role there and even to the extent that it does feature it imposes scarcely any restriction on the receiver's room for manoeuvre.

37. *Cf.*, for example, BAG 20.11.1970, *NJW* 1971, 774 and BAG 17.9.1974, *NJW* 1975, 182.
38. Kania T., *loc. cit.*, p. 834.
39. Such *Betriebsvereinbarungen* can, however, always be terminated with three months' notice even if they had been concluded for a longer period. On the basis of §120 InsO they can be terminated even earlier than this if there is just cause for doing so.
40. Strothmann Y. and Rendels D., *loc. cit.*, p. 156.
41. Opinions are divided on this, given that the treatment of the *Interessenausgleich* does not include all the aspects covered by this preliminary testing, such as notice periods and specific bans on dismissal; see, on this point, Duwell J., *op. cit.*, p. 1120. See Chapter 4, Section 2 above on the preliminary testing of dismissals.

Specific participation as regards the actual bankruptcy petition is lacking in three of the four countries. Only under Belgian law is it expressly stipulated that the works council must be given notification of the petition. An indirect obligation to inform the *Betriebsrat* also exists in Germany via the latter's general right to information. In The Netherlands, however, the employer's decision to submit a bankruptcy petition himself is not subject to the works council's consultation right (*adviesrecht*) ex art. 25 WOR.

As regards participation by the works council in the event of collective dismissals and business transfers following a bankruptcy judgment, it may be said that although in Belgium and The Netherlands this must, in theory, be observed by the receiver just as the employer must do prior to a bankruptcy, such participation plays scarcely any role in practice. In Germany, on the other hand, participation rights in the event of collective dismissals and business transfers – including in bankruptcy situations – had been so rigorously established that this was considered to represent a major obstacle to corporate rescues and business transfers in the context of bankruptcy. As a consequence, the introduction of the current *Insolvenzordnung* has substantially weakened these rights as regards their applicability to the receiver in a bankruptcy situation. This has, in a sense, brought the situation in Germany in line with that in Belgium and The Netherlands.

7. Conclusions

In the past in Europe a bankruptcy was always seen as a tragic event both for the (legal) person concerned and for the latter's creditors. Nowadays it often happens that a bankruptcy is a mere technical operation to liberate a group of companies of divisions that are no longer competitive. Furthermore there is a rising tendency in the European countries to adopt a somewhat less critical view of bankruptcy and to see it more as the unavoidable "fallout" of a society where high-risk entrepreneurship is valued and encouraged, as in the USA.[1]

All this can not efface the hardship of a bankruptcy to the employees, who were dependent upon the bankrupt not only for their income but also for their employment and social security. The extent to which these employees retain their prospects in a bankruptcy situation is determined by the applicable law.

In order to put the situation as it exists in The Netherlands into perspective, in the present study a comparison is made between the law on the matter in The Netherlands and that in its neighbouring countries: Belgium, Germany and Britain.

For the purposes of assessing the situation as it exists under Netherlands law from an employee's point of view, ten "indicators" have been chosen for scrutiny in this study:

1. the ranking of pay claims dating from after a bankruptcy judgment (Chapter 2, Section 2);
2. the ranking of pay claims dating from prior to a bankruptcy judgment (Chapter 2, Section 3)
3. the settlement of claims by guarantee institutions and the limitation of such guarantees (Chapter 2, Section 2);
4. the financing of guarantee schemes (Chapter 3, Section 4);
5. protection against dismissal, primarily in cases of selective dismissal (Chapter 4, Sections 2–4 and 7);
6. notice periods (Chapter 4, Section 5);
7. forms of compensation for dismissal and redundancy payments (Chapter 4, Section 6);
8. business transfers in the context of bankruptcy (Chapter 5);
9. participation rights as regards a bankruptcy petition (Chapter 6, Section 2),
10. participation rights as regards post-bankruptcy decisions made by the receiver (Chapter 6, Section 3).

---

1. *Cf.* the Note "De ondernemende samenleving" by EZ (Bijl. Hand. T.K. 1998–99, 26 736, no. 1).

R. Blanpain, A.T.J.M. Jacobs (eds.), Employee Rights in Bankruptcy, 63–70.

With respect to each of these indicators, on the basis of our study of the different legal systems each of the four countries has been placed in first, second, third or fourth position according to the degree of "favourability" of that particular system towards the interests of the employees affected by bankruptcy. In some instances the differences between one or other legal systems are in our view negligible and they occupy an equal position. This is shown as 1–2, 1–3, 1–4, 2–3, 2–4 or 3–4 and the findings concerned are counted as 1½, 2, 2½, 3 and 3½.

	The Netherlands	Belgium	Germany	Britain
Ranking of pay claims dating from after a bankruptcy judgment	2	3–4	1	3–4
Ranking of pay claims dating from before a bankruptcy judgment	1–4	1–4	1–4	1–4
Settlement of claims by guarantee institutions and applicable limitations	1–2	3–4	1–2	3–4
Financing of guarantee institutions	4	1–3	1–3	1–3
Protection against dismissal	2–3	4	1	2–3
notice periods	4	1	2	3
Forms of compensation for dismissal and redundancy payments	4	1	2	3
Business transfers in the context of bankruptcy	4	1	2–3	2–3
Participation rights as regards a bankruptcy petition	2–3	1	2–3	4
Participation rights as regards post-bankruptcy decisions by the receiver	2–3	2–3	1	4
Total	29.5	22	18	30.5

All in all this leads us to the conclusion that, in the mutual relations between the four legal systems studied, Germany and Belgium are the most favourable towards employees affected by a bankruptcy situation and The Netherlands and Britain offer them the least.[2] Therefore the Dutch bankruptcy expert Knüppe seems quite right when he described the Dutch bankruptcy law as an "employer's Valhalla".[3]

The bankruptcy of a (legal) person who operates a company represents a serious blow to the secure livelihood and legal position of its employees. No legislation, however, can ever neutralize these effects entirely: an inevitable area of tension exists between the financing-techniques extreme of minimum employee protection that allows the most profitable corporate rescue and the equalization-approach extreme of maximum employee protection that spells doom for any chances of successful corporate rescue. At best, legislation can

2. The above table and method of calculation is, of course, open to the criticism that not every indicator carries equal importance. In our view, however, assigning a weighting factor to each indicator to overcome this merely produces a spurious impression of accuracy. Furthermore, it ultimately does nothing to alter the wide gap between The Netherlands (and, to a lesser extent, British) position on the one hand and the German and Belgian position on the other, since The Netherlands system comes bottom for half of the indicators and scores on the low side even for the others.
3. See Knüppe B.F.M., in : A.M. Luttmer-Kat (ed.), *op. cit.*, p. 53.

attempt to ease the distress where possible by seeking out the well-known "golden mean". Our findings indicate that the Dutch legislators, as compared with those in the other countries studied (particularly Belgium and Germany), still have some way to go before arriving at such a "golden mean" position.

Unfortunately, a revision of employee rights in bankruptcy in The Netherlands is actually complicated by the fact that bankruptcy law in Europe is developing along different lines. In some important countries, like Britain, there are different forms of bankruptcy procedure, which still have clearly separate functions. The winding-up procedure is not appropriate for a "re-start" following bankruptcy, one reason being that pay claims dating from after the bankruptcy petition are given low preference. Consequently, there is more of a tendency to use – where a corporate rescue is being contemplated – the receivership procedure, which makes it easier to sell off a company as a going concern.

In Germany, in the new *Insolvenzordnung* composition procedures (the former *Vergleichsverfahren*: *cf.* The Netherlands *surséance van betaling* [judicial leave to suspend payment of debts]) and discharge procedures (the former *Konkursverfahren*: *cf.* The Netherlands *faillissement* [bankruptcy]) have been combined into a single *Insolvenzverfahren*.

These contrasting German and British models have called for a fundamental re-think on the difference between the *surséance* and bankruptcy procedures provided for in The Netherlands. Should it be recommended that the two be combined in imitation of the German model, as actually suggested by Bloemarts?[4] And if so, what level should be set for employee protection? At the current high level provided for in the case of *surséance van betaling,* at the low level provided for in the event of bankruptcy, or somewhere in between? Or should the British model be followed, which could entail deciding to make the *surséance van betaling* procedure more particularly suited to corporate rescue and restructuring attempts and to reserve bankruptcy to actual liquidations? This could be done by somewhat weakening the current – still in some respects very strong – protection provided for employees in a *surséance van betaling* context and strengthening the currently very weak position of employees in a bankruptcy context.[5]

Up until now the Dutch legislator has avoided a clear choice between the British and the German approach. Recent bills sent to parliament were limited to mere technical and partial amendments of the existing system.

This raises the associated issue of the manner in which the employer's liabilities towards the employee should be secured. Although some see it as a specific responsibility of the public authorities, the politicians throw this particular ball back into the court of employers and employees. And if there is a responsibility for the public authorities, again various solutions are conceivable. One way is an improvement of the standing of workers' claims in bankruptcy law itself. The alternative way is to improve the guarantee of employees' pay claims under existing public guarantee schemes.

4. Bloemarts J.C.M.G., in: A.M. Luttmer-Kat (ed.), *op. cit.*, p. 76.
5. Bloemarts J.C.M.G., in: A.M. Luttmer-Kat (ed.), *op. cit.*, p. 77.

It is apparent from Chapter 2 of this study that, although the pay claims of a bankrupt employer's employees dating from the period immediately before the bankruptcy judgment are classed as "preferential", in all four of the countries studied this preference counts for very little. Usually, the estate has insufficient assets to effect such payment to the employees. Often the estate does not even have enough to effect all the post-bankruptcy debts.

Therefore it seems evident that the pay claims of employees are best served by the second way: to improve the guarantee of employees' pay claims under independent public guarantee schemes.

However, this makes the first way, the revision of the priorities under bankruptcy law, not entirely without importance. The assignment of priority under bankruptcy law is important for the guarantee institutions, since it determines their chances of claiming back as much as possible of the payments they made. It means that in those bankruptcies in which there are still assets left, the guarantee institutions can recover more than under the actual situation. This will have a downward effect on the contributions they have to impose.

And specific for The Netherlands there is the argument, that the priorities for pre-bankruptcy-claims are also determining the ranking of post-bankruptcy claims against the estate. So a better ranking in the pre-bankruptcy claims may bring the employees or the guarantee institutions more fruits even in cases in which there is nothing left to pay off pre-bankruptcy debts.

As is apparent from Chapter 3 in all four of the countries studied and perfectly in line with the European Directive, the existing rules have substantially limited the liability for the pay claims of the employees of these guarantee institutions, both in terms of temporal limits on the claims for which they guarantee payment and in terms of the nature of these claims. Ceilings are also set on the amounts that are paid. Although in comparative terms, the situation in The Netherlands on this aspect is in fact the best (ranking equally with Germany), it must be born in mind that employees in The Netherlands – in contrast to those in the other countries – have to contribute half of the costs of this scheme themselves. So for The Netherlands it may be argued that this co-financing by employees should be compensated by an extension of the period covered by the guarantee or also to include forms of compensation for dismissal within its scope.

However, other items should be considered as well. In all countries studied "tertiary" terms and conditions of employment in particular, such as forms of compensation for dismissal, supplementary social security, pension contributions, etc., mostly seem to be excluded from the category of pay claims for which the guarantee institutions accept liability. As a result of these restrictions, many of the employees' acquired rights still come to nothing in a bankruptcy situation.

Such claims could be catered for in the context of a fund set up for each industry or branch of activity to assume responsibility for the risk of insolvency. A second possibility would be for every employee to be individually insured – whether paid for by the employer or not – against the risk of his employer's insolvency. Lastly, there is the possibility of a statutory scheme whereby those of the employer's assets to which the employee has an outstanding claim are separated out from the bankruptcy procedure. However, since this offers no solution in cases involving an estate that possesses no assets, the sums involved have to be made external to the business. This can be done in a manner similar to that in which pensions and early retirement pensions are (compulsorily) secured.

Along with the loss of outstanding pay entitlements, the great risk for employees of a bankrupt company is the threat of losing their jobs. This is because the protection offered by normal dismissals law dwindles away in a bankruptcy situation. One of the striking features here is that this withdrawal of protection is most conspicuous in the event of complete company closure entailing dismissal of the entire workforce. Also, the decline in protection is the more serious the stronger normal dismissals law is in the country concerned. This means that the relative loss of protection is only minor in Belgium and Britain, where protection against dismissal in normal situations outside bankruptcy is already limited.

In Germany, where a relatively extensive degree of protection against dismissal exists, the legislation, until recently, was aimed at continuing to maintain that protection in bankruptcy situations. Recently, however, the introduction of the current *Insolvenzordnung* has marked a withdrawal from that position and a considerable restriction of the relevant protection against dismissal, albeit still not to so extreme an extent as in The Netherlands.

In The Netherlands, which has the most rigorously protective dismissals law of all the countries studied, the worsening of protection against dismissal in case of a bankruptcy is most drastic. Notice periods, in particular, are shorter in The Netherlands than in any of the three other countries studied, and forms of financial compensation for employees such as severance payments are similarly minimal, whereas the German system demonstrates that less drastic restrictions on protection against dismissal in bankruptcy situations are not necessarily unrealistic.

It is notable that, as a result, in The Netherlands bankruptcy appears to have developed into an alternative strategy for circumventing normal dismissals law, as may be deduced from the number of so-called "re-starts" (*doorstarts*) via which, following bankruptcy, many companies prosper once again.

The greatest hope for employees in a bankruptcy situation lies in the possible transfer of the business to a new owner. However, potential purchasers might be deterred by the prospect of being saddled with too many debts inherited from the bankrupt company and having to take over its entire workforce. Consequently, when in 1977 the EC issued its Directive 77/187 (amended in 1998 by Directive 98/50 and consolidated by Directive 2001/23) making these consequences the norm in the event of a normal business transfer, it allowed for an exception in the case of transfers effectuated during bankruptcy proceedings. This opportunity of exempting bankruptcy-related transfers from the rules has been used in their respective legislative by all four of the Member States studied here, and more extensively so in The Netherlands than in the three other countries. In Belgium and Britain, although the general rules on business transfers are deemed non-applicable in bankruptcy situations, once a business has been transferred following a bankruptcy judgment the transferee is required to apply the principles of the transfer regulations to some extent with respect to the employees transferred to him. In Germany, although the general rules on business transfers have recently been curtailed to some degree, on the main issues the rules remain applicable to bankruptcy-related transfers.

Here again, in comparison with the other legal systems studied the interpretation given to the European Directive in The Netherlands seems somewhat drastic. Apart from the consequent possibility of only some employees being transferred, the total exclusion of the automatic transfer of the employees to the new company leaves the way wide open for former contractually agreed conditions to be entirely ignored.

Considering the regular occurrence of "re-starts" following bankruptcy, it may be asked whether The Netherlands has perhaps been altogether too drastic in its exclusion of the Directive's provisions in the event of bankruptcy.

In case of a transfer of the undertaking out of a bankruptcy situation it frequently happens that not all the employees of the bankrupt enterprise are taken over. In those cases the fate of the employees that are not taken over is the harshest. The existing arrangements for the temporary support of employees dismissed by the receiver in a bankruptcy situation are normally very poor. Everyone expresses awareness of the individual harm suffered, not only in financial but also in non-material terms, by those employees for whom there is no place in the re-started company. The question arises: how best to avoid the harm suffered by those employees who are the losers in a bankruptcy situation?

The best remedy, of course, is to find alternative employment as quickly as possible for these employees who have lost out. This represents a priority for both the receiver and the public authorities. For the receiver, because doing so enables him to limit as far as possible the liabilities or expenses incurred for the estate in connection with the dismissals he carries out. And for the public authorities (local, regional or national), because as guardians of the public interest, in the event of large-scale dismissals they are responsible for avoiding the disruption of a particular community.

In so far as new jobs cannot be found quickly for the dismissed employees, a certain amount of financial assistance mitigates the hardship to some extent. In The Netherlands some authors have proposed that the receiver in bankruptcy should also be required to pay some form of compensation for dismissal deriving from his handling of the situation.[6] This compensation

6. *Cf.* Grapperhaus F.B.J., in: A.M. Luttmer-Kat (ed.), *op. cit.*, p. 72, who nevertheless favours imposing a ceiling on compensation for dismissal, since any other approach always proves less appropriate and possibly disproportionately unfavourable to the other creditors.

should also qualify for guaranteed payment under the existing guarantee institutions schemes.

A strong argument for this plea can be found in ILO-Convention No. 173 on the protection of employees' claims in the event of their employers' insolvency. According to this convention "severance pays due to workers upon termination of their employment" are to be included among the employees' claims, which should be given preference over ordinary claims and/or secured by a guarantee institution set up for the payment of these claims (art. 6 and 12).

Although there is thus a convenient tendency to see responsibility for this – and hence its financing – as lying with the public authorities, it is doubtful whether in the present-day circumstances in The Netherlands this is politically feasible.

Yet, the urgency of this demand was illustrated in The Netherlands most notably in the 1990s in the case of the DAF bankruptcy, in which a solidarity fund was established to provide for supplementary financial assistance. This fund, the Stichting Ondersteuningsfonds Oud-Werknemers DAF, was to a large extent financed by those employees who were taken over by the restarted company DAF Trucks.

However, to opt for a system whereby those employees who keep their jobs help to finance a benevolent fund calls for a very strong feeling of solidarity. In practice, this proved possible for as long as the employees in question still did not know whether or not they would be among the fortunate ones. Once the selection had been made, however, some of the employees who had kept their jobs turned out to have difficulty in accepting their obligation to hand over part of their pay to the DAF solidarity Funds. Solidarity therefore needs to be established in good time, and in any event before it is known who is and who is not being transferred. Also, this method is workable only in cases where a sufficiently large number of employees are transferred to the new company, because otherwise there will not be an adequate financial basis for a benevolent fund.

Finally a word on employee participation. The study made here demonstrates that the whole idea of employee participation is difficult to reconcile with bankruptcy. However, in Belgium and Germany an attempt has nevertheless been made to preserve the rules on participation wherever possible in bankruptcy situations. In The Netherlands, however, employee participation with respect to the bankruptcy petition has become, in practice, all but a dead letter. And during the bankruptcy proceedings receivers, for pragmatic reasons, usually involve employees' representatives in their plans but reserve ultimate decision-making powers to themselves. Surely participation merits better treatment. The owner of a company undergoing financial difficulties should provide employee representatives in good time with information and judges should involve them in the process of deciding on the bankruptcy petition. Receivers should notify them and keep them up-to-date on the state of affairs as intensive as possible.